**published by
altiorapeto**

© Paul B Davies 2016

The moral rights of the author have been asserted

All rights reserved

This publication may not be reproduced or transmitted, in whole or in part, in any form or by any means, now known or hereafter invented, without the prior permission in writing of the author or as expressly permitted by law

ISBN 978-1-5262-0593-3

# JOHN JONAS

# VICTORIAN POLICEMAN

Paul B Davies

# PREFACE

In taking the journey back into time which is involved in discovering family history, like most people, I didn't come across anything particularly unexpected, with one exception, which is the subject of this book.

Having discovered the end of a trail in North Yorkshire, or the North Riding as it then was, a casual internet search, for a name I'd found, led to Essex and Suffolk, and the outline of a story which was something of a surprise. That however was only the beginning, as I became increasingly intrigued by the individual concerned, and about the police forces, then in their infancy, that he'd been part of.

Contemporary newspapers were useful in discovering more, but while coverage can be extensive it is often inconsistent. Reporting could be highly localised, although the name and/or geographical distribution of a paper might suggest otherwise. Often newspapers reported only what they had space for and/or what they thought would interest their readers (and then obviously, only if a story had been 'filed'). The style and extent of accounts also change over time, and of course the usual reporting pattern could be significantly distorted by a 'major' news event.

Coverage therefore not only has to be read with the 'usual caution', but also with the realisation that even significant stories may not have been reported, and that what was published could be far from comprehensive.

Although obviously dependent on what documents were originally produced, and then what was archived, County Record Offices were another useful source.

Libraries, for books as well as newspapers, were invaluable.

Eventually a biography of my subject began to emerge and from that the idea of this book evolved. Inevitably, as it had a significant impact on much of his life, this includes some of the early history of the police forces involved – readers who might be interested in this aspect of the book should particularly refer to notes with emboldened numbers. However, I hope that these readers will appreciate that I've had to resist the temptation to pursue lines of enquiry unrelated to the biography.

I've obviously tried to be as accurate as possible, and have been as comprehensive as I believe the narrative requires, but hope that readers who identify any errors or omissions will forgive me (and let me know), as I hope that readers who might have additional information about John Jonas will also contact me: johnjonas@paulbdavies.plus.com

# ACKNOWLEDGEMENTS

Thanks to Robert Aconley, Julie Allenby, Darren Armstrong, Beck Isle Museum, Alice Bennett, John Blanchard, Maureen Braithwaite, the British Library, Bury St Edmunds Record Office, Ann Church, Andrew Clarke, Gordon Clitheroe, Philip and Sue Combes, Jacqueline Cooper, Darlington Library, Essex Police Museum, Essex Record Office (ERO), Fred Feather, Alan Fitch, Gloucestershire Archive (GA), Samantha George, Robert Green, Elaine Hickes, Karim Hussain, Jane Ingle, Pauline Lancaster, Hannah Lincoln, Ralph Lindley, Malton Library, Martin Lockwood, Metropolitan Police Heritage Centre, Clare McCluskey, Sara McGinlay, Geoff Myers, Norfolk Library Service, North York Moors Railway, North Yorkshire County Record Office (NYCRO), Ann Parkinson, Ralph Phillips, Christina Pierce-Winters, Police History Society, Redcar Library, Ripon Museum Trust, Heather Robb, Katie Robinson, Joanne Rogers, Ryedale Family History Group, Diana Sadler, Peter Sanders, Scarborough Library, Sally-Ann Shearn, Mark Sissons, Maddie Smith, the Sydney Jones Library, Martin Stallion, Sarah Steggles, Stockton Library, Paul Terry, Rob Wake and Becky Wash and to any others I've accidentally missed or somehow overlooked.

# CONTENTS

| | |
|---|---|
| Lavenham | 11 |
| The Essex Constabulary | 17 |
| Rural Essex (Halstead, Foxearth, Sible Hedingham, Southminster and Stansted Mountfitchet) | 23 |
| The North Riding Constabulary | 39 |
| Pickering Lythe | 43 |
| Constabulary Duties | 55 |
| Misadventure (Welburn and South Stockton) | 59 |
| New Start | 67 |
| Cropton | 93 |
| Return to Normal? | 107 |
| Notes | 119 |
| Sources | 183 |
| Index | 189 |

# LAVENHAM

In the early 19$^{th}$ century, the medieval town of Lavenham, in south-west Suffolk, consisted of only a few streets around a small market area. The High Street formed part of the road between Sudbury, some 8 miles south-west, to Bury St Edmunds, 12 miles north-west; while Water Street formed the beginning of the road to Hadleigh, around 10 miles south-east. The relatively short Prentice, Bolton, Barn and Lady Streets radiated east and south from the central Market Place; Shilling Street, between Bolton and Water Streets, ran parallel to Barn Street. Church Street, which also formed part of the road to Sudbury, connected the junction of Water Street and High Street to the disproportionately large parish church (of Saints Peter and Paul). The latter had been funded mainly with profits from the wool trade, particularly wool combing which had made Lavenham relatively prosperous in the 17$^{th}$ and 18$^{th}$ centuries, but which was in decline by this time.[1]

The town was relatively self-contained with Attorney, Blacksmith, Bricklayer, Butcher, Carpenter, Carrier, Chemist, Cooper, Glover, Gunsmith, Hairdresser, Ironmonger, Painter, Plumber, Publican, Rope Maker, School Master, Shoemaker, Shopkeeper, Surgeon, Tailor, Thatcher, Wheelwright and Watch Maker among the occupations of the 1,871 population recorded by the 1841 Census.

John Jonas was baptised in the parish church in July 1818. His parents were recorded as Charles and Ann but the circumstances raise some doubt in regard to the former.

As their marriage occurred less than five weeks before John's baptism it's likely that either John had already been born or that Ann was at a very advanced stage of pregnancy, so theirs may have been a marriage of 'convenience'.[2] Many years later John gave his father's name as Emanuel (Jonas).[3]

The location of John's baptism suggests that the family lived in Lavenham, but by 1831, when John was around 13, it seems that their home was in Preston St Mary, around two miles east, north-east of the town.[4] This was a small settlement where unsurprisingly the major source of employment was agriculture or related support services, such as blacksmith and wheelwright.[5] However, with most other services absent, the village would have been reliant on Lavenham. It was the largest settlement in the area, with a regular market and shops, and the Jonas's had many members of the extended family living there.[6]

The Jonas's home was likely to have been no more than two or three rooms in a small cottage, which probably lacked any other facilities.[7]

Charles's income would have fluctuated with the seasons, and John and his mother may have had to contribute in whatever way they could; possibly through seasonal work on the land and/or casual employment, probably in Lavenham. John therefore may not have had time for any education, other than that he might have received at Sunday school. However, as an only child, it's possible that he wasn't required to work all of the time, and that his parents could sometimes afford school, so he may have received some education at either the *British* or the *National* school in Lavenham.[8]

It may even have been the case that a relative, such as his paternal uncle Henry (a wool comber) or his paternal aunt Eliza (and/or her husband) helped to pay for some education.

Recognising the material benefits of a 'trade', perhaps in the homes of Henry and Eliza, may eventually have led John into shoe making, as in 1841 he was described as a cordwainer. By then he was possibly 23 and had probably been employed at this for the previous couple of years.[9] Before that he was likely to have completed an apprenticeship, of up to seven years, so might have been 14 or younger when he began learning how to make shoes.[10]

Given the consistency in the 1851 and 1861 Censuses, and the otherwise improbable likelihood of the location, it seems reasonable to believe that the birthplace of Eleanor Gee was Thomastown in County Kilkenny (now Eire). It's likely that Eleanor met and married Robert Deacon, Dakin or Daking, in Ireland, probably in 1811.[11]

Their daughter Eleanor, baptised at Lavenham in May 1816, was the second oldest surviving of nine Deacon children.[12]

With the uncertainty, and probable paucity, of her father's income, as a tinker, it's likely that the family home was as, if not more sparse than that of the Jonas's.[13] It's also probably the reason that Eleanor was unlikely to have received an education, and to have begun working at an early age.[14] The importance of her income to the family may explain why she was probably around 19 before she married John Jonas, in Lavenham in July 1835.[15]

There is no civil record of the birth of John and Eleanor's daughter, Eleanor (Ann) or son, John (George) but their baptisms were recorded in Lavenham in November 1837.[16] Surprisingly, because according to later records he was younger, John was baptised a fortnight before his sister.[17] Although there could be many reasons for this it's possible that his mother may have been unwell when pregnant with John, which had caused her and his father to delay the baptism of their daughter; or that there'd been fears for John's survival, leading to an early baptism, with his sister being baptised only after he'd made a 'recovery'.[18]

By this time the economy had entered what came to be recognised as the most severe economic depression of the century and John may have realised that future opportunities in Lavenham were limited.[19] However they wouldn't have been able to search for alternatives until John finished his apprenticeship, which was probably during the summer of 1839.[20]

Most people at this time spent their lives in the place where they'd been born and grown up, and mobility was relatively limited.[21] However John and Eleanor may have been encouraged by, or invited to follow, other members of the family, for example John's uncle Henry, who in 1841 was living in Portland Place, Lakenham, Norwich.

By then Eleanor and her children were living in nearby Carmen's Buildings, and as the birth of a second son, Alfred (James), had been registered in Lakenham in January 1840, they may have been there since leaving Lavenham. Although the other twenty four 'families', who also lived in Carmen's Buildings, all seem to have been employed in some way, the accommodation was likely to have been amongst the poorest available.[22]

Unusually for a married woman, an occupation (shoe maker) was also recorded for Eleanor, so unless her Census entry should have read shoe makers wife, she may have been helping to maximise the family income by making the shoes while John secured the orders for them. However, it's equally possible that there was an error by, or a misunderstanding on the part of the Census enumerator, or that Eleanor had some other motive for wanting to be regarded as employed.

Whatever the explanation, with significant everyday domestic demands, a potentially 'hostile' environment, a baby and two relatively young children to be cared for, life for Eleanor must have been fraught. It shouldn't be surprising therefore that this situation, together with increasing competition from factory produced footwear, probably leading to an increasingly erratic and uncertain income, persuaded John to consider an occupation other than the one which he'd probably spent years learning.

# THE ESSEX CONSTABULARY

The movement towards a consistently organised national police structure had begun largely as the result of fear of rising crime, leading to the formation, in 1829, of the Metropolitan Police. In contrast to previous arrangements this was a force of permanent, full time, regularly paid, uniformed Constables.

From 1835, Boroughs had been expected to form forces and, in response to the Chartist movement, in 1839 the concept was extended to rural areas.[23]

Walking the lanes of Norfolk, in search of orders for shoes, John would have probably begun meeting members of the new county Constabulary, particularly as they may have challenged him as a possible vagrant or poacher.

He may have already witnessed the impact of the 'new' police locally, in Hadleigh, where a former Metropolitan Police officer had been employed under the auspices of the 1833 Lighting and Watching Act.[24] He may also have begun to notice advertisements seeking recruits. As the family's situation possibly worsened, the regular pay and other benefits in the Constabulary must have seemed increasingly attractive.[25]

West Suffolk, where John and Eleanor had grown up, hadn't established a Constabulary, and he may not have been tall enough for Norfolk.[26]

He could of course have joined a Borough force but, besides none other than Sudbury being reasonably close to Lavenham, may have recognised the limitations of these compared with the county forces.[27]

The alternative was Essex, which John and Eleanor may have hoped would present an opportunity, in the northern part of the county, close to Lavenham. John probably applied to join the force early in 1842, when further expansion was anticipated.

Fortunately, as measured during his recruitment, John was at least half an inch (13mm) taller than the required minimum 5'7" (1.71m).[28] He was obviously also able to satisfy the other entrance requirements, proving to be generally intelligent, literate (and able to keep accounts) and in good health, with a strong constitution.[29] Additionally, he must have been able to provide a reference (possibly from the cordwainer he'd been apprenticed to) which vouched for his honesty, sobriety, conduct and temperament, over at least the previous five years.

After his physical condition was presumably found to be acceptable, John was sworn in on 22 April.[30] He may have been a shoe maker from a small Suffolk town but John wouldn't have been out of place among the 105 Constables who then formed the Essex Constabulary.[31] Recruits were from a wide range of occupations, including clerks, craftsmen, labourers, shop assistants and soldiers, many from outside the county.[32]

Initially, John would have spent some time in Chelmsford, probably mostly learning what was expected of him when patrolling a 'guard' (beat).[33]

However, with their normal duties also to be performed, this was probably about all that the Superintendent, Inspector and ten Constables, then stationed in Chelmsford, could be expected to have time to pass on (particularly bearing in mind that during 1842 some 133 men, or an average of 11 per month, were sworn in).[34]

Possibly to compensate for the limited tuition, but more probably in anticipation of a future posting without colleagues and/or superiors in proximity, John would have been given a copy of *Orders and Instructions Framed and Issued for the Superintendents and Constables of the Essex Constabulary*.[35]

This was a comprehensive handbook which would have been essential to John, and his colleagues, in performing their duties. However, it would also shape their lives as it not only covered operational issues but also terms and conditions and behavioural expectations.

In May, John was sent to his first operational posting, in Halstead. As this probably signified the end of his induction, and the beginning of his new role, it was when he was most likely to have been provided with a uniform. This consisted of a single breasted royal blue 'coat' with an embroidered (crown and number) collar, blue 'dress' and 'undress' trousers, greatcoat, cape, boots, shoes and a black 'stove pipe' (top) hat.[36] In addition he would have been issued with a wooden rattle (to raise the alarm), a baton (sometimes referred to as a truncheon or staff) and a pair of (figure of eight) handcuffs. Constables were expected to supply their own pen and notebook (for documenting patrols, arrests, court appearances and the like), as well as some sort of 'knapsack' for carrying everything.[37]

It's likely that Eleanor and the children had moved to Chelmsford when John joined the force as they probably wouldn't otherwise have had any money, the family in Lavenham was unlikely to have been able to accommodate them and, with his expected attendance pattern, John wouldn't have been able to travel to them. However, moving wouldn't have been as difficult as might be imagined, as the family were unlikely to have had many personal belongings or household chattels. With the majority of accommodation rented on weekly or monthly tenancies, relocation, at least from a practical point of view, was likely to have been relatively straightforward. Now, although another move was required, the family could probably look forward to some domestic stability, underpinned by a Constable 3$^{rd}$ class's salary of 17s (85p) per week.[38]

Halstead, with a population almost three times that of Lavenham, was some 14 miles south-west of the latter, via Sudbury.[39] It was situated on either side of the valley of the River Colne, along a road from London to Bury St Edmund's and another between Colchester and Cambridge. The inns, shops and dwellings which formed the town lined several streets, with the wide High Street, ascending gently from the river to the church, being most prominent. There was considerable employment in textile manufacturing although, as in other towns in this area of Essex and Suffolk, many found work as straw platters.

Having been a Petty Sessions Division of the Hinckford Hundred, Halstead was now part of the Essex Constabulary South Hinckford Division.[40] Despite the town having one of the few police stations in the county the Superintendent in charge of the Division was based at Braintree, around 7 miles to the south-west.[41]

However, Halstead had an Inspector and working with him, in a police station, in proximity to a (Petty Sessions) court must have provided ideal experience for a new Constable.[42]

John would also have benefitted from working with a second Constable, who was stationed at Halstead from time to time, and alongside a local (parish) constable, who was active in the town during this period.

In locations where there were several officers, and significant residential and/or commercial development, Constables may have spent at least several hours, if not all of their time on duty, patrolling a particular 'guard', but otherwise it seems reasonable to believe that activities would have been tailored to the requirements of the area and to the resources available. So, as part of a small team, with a police station to 'cover', John would probably only have spent part of his time patrolling.

The time when it was to be undertaken, and the route and features of a 'guard' are likely to have determined how long it took to complete.[43] John, and his colleagues, therefore probably undertook a mixture of patrols, of varying durations, in the town or in the surrounding area, particularly to the south and west of Halstead. Although some of these may have been during the daytime, the patrolling likely to have been considered most effective was that after dark, so John's working day may have been spread around a large part of the clock, and would have been repeated every day of the week (and every week of the year).

With little or no street lighting, patrols in the town would have been difficult, but a total absence of lighting and unmade roads would have made those in the rural areas even more so.[44]

To help overcome at least the lighting problem, Constable Jonas would have been issued with a large 'bulls eye' lens oil lamp.[45]

John's other duties would probably have mainly involved following up something which had come, or been brought, to his attention while on patrol, or assisting his Inspector or colleague(s) in some way. Probably his most significant and regular other duty would have been sharing 'coverage' of the police station, particularly when any prisoners were being held. This was the case one Saturday in May 1843 when John discovered, that in the hour since he'd last checked, some prisoners had escaped through a hole made in the wall of their cell.

Fortunately, he managed to recapture one of the escapees within an hour, while colleagues apprehended two of the others during the following few hours. However, one remained at large and the episode may have had lasting repercussions for Constable Jonas.[46]

# RURAL ESSEX

John was promoted to Constable 2$^{nd}$ class on 1$^{st}$ October 1843.[47] This may have been in recognition of him completing a period of probation, or because he was being 'removed' to Foxearth, in the neighbouring North Hinckford Division.[48] Although such transfers were essentially compulsory, and those who didn't want to move had to resign, or were dismissed, for the majority they were no doubt an expected part of being a policeman.

As well as vacancies created by the relatively high personnel 'turnover' then prevailing others would have arisen as the Establishment (the authorised and funded number of each rank) increased with the development of the force. Some probably also came about as the distribution of posts was refined (based on crime patterns, as well as the location of police stations/lock ups).[49]

It seems likely that those seeking transfers, and/or promotions, would generally have welcomed 'removals'.

Although John's promotion meant a salary increase of 2s (10p) per week, the family may not have experienced any marked change or 'improvement' in their domestic circumstances particularly if the available accommodation wasn't significantly different from where they'd been living. Rents would typically have been around 3s, or later 4s (15 or 20p) per week, although the family probably also had other 'unavoidable' commitments such as membership of some sort of benefits club or society, in case of ill health, incapacity and/or death.[50]

They may also have made contributions to the church and payments for education, particularly the latter as while living in Foxearth, children Eleanor, John and Alfred were in, or entered, their potential school years. Their attendance may have been encouraged (or thwarted) by the birth of John and Eleanor's second daughter, Julia (Ann), in June 1847.[51]

Foxearth, around 7 miles south-west of Lavenham, was mainly clustered around the junction of a local road and another between Sudbury, and Cavendish to the north-west. Although the population was relatively small, there were facilities in the village for all of the family's immediate needs, and Sudbury was only around 4 miles south-east if anything more was required.[52]

The Divisional Superintendent was based, around 9 miles to the south-west, at Castle Hedingham.

For the first time in his police career, John wouldn't have had colleagues and/or superiors in proximity which, although novel for him, was the usual arrangement in rural Essex at this time.

Constable Jonas's duties in Foxearth probably mostly involved patrolling, but on occasions he would also have had to arrest people, or to deliver summonses for: assault, breaking (labour) contracts, cruelty to animals, drunkenness, failure to pay rates or support for a child or a family; riding without reins or in some manner dangerously, theft or wilful damage.

He would also have intercepted poachers, moved on travellers and vagrants, observed potential crime scenes and, occasionally, assisted colleagues elsewhere.

The few incidents reported which involved John were relatively minor - theft of hay in March 1845 (twelve months' hard labour) and of apples, by 12 and 13 year old brothers, in October 1847 (one months' and six months' hard labour).[53]

As in the area around Halstead, Constable Jonas's patrols would have included outlying farms and houses, and it was while doing this in Pentlow, around 2 miles north-west of Foxearth, one night in December 1847, that he encountered three men. He managed to capture one of them, and on searching him found a crow (wrecking) bar, two sacks, matches and candles, all of which would have been useful in burgling property – later at Castle Hedingham Petty Sessions the man was sentenced to three months' in Chelmsford gaol.[54]

Occasionally, there were more unusual incidents, such as in February 1848, when Constable Jonas had to investigate the death of a man killed by a farm cart tipping on to him, after it had collided with an oncoming wagon, on a dark morning.[55]

While remaining a Constable 2nd class, in June 1849 John was 'removed' to Sible Hedingham and at the Census, in March 1851, was living with his family (and mother in law) on Swan Street, the main road through the village.[56]

Located in the Colne Valley, around 14 miles south-west of Lavenham, Sible Hedingham had a population slightly larger than that of the latter and as a result was similarly self-contained with inns, shops and schools.[57]

Although relatively mobile from a domestic point of view the family must have begun to resent these relocations.

As well as the upheaval involved in moving home, they meant losing friends and, in the case of the eldest children, at least changing if not finishing school.

As a purpose built police station had opened on Queen Street (which led to Sible Hedingham, around two thirds of a mile away) in Castle Hedingham in early 1844, for John the most significant aspect of the move was probably a return to daily reporting to a police station and, as in Halstead, carrying out duties at the latter.[58] By this time these included processing any vagrants as from earlier that year Essex Constabulary had begun taking on the role of assistant Relieving Officers for the local Poor Law Unions.[59]

Such developments may have been the catalyst for the publication that summer of *Orders and Instructions Framed and Issued for the Government of the Essex Constabulary*. This updated and added considerably to the previous *Orders and ...*, not only from an operational point of view, but also in regard to officers' everyday lives.[60]

Apart from police station commitments, duty in Sible Hedingham was probably little different from Foxearth. John was involved in cases of theft of barley in August 1849 (twelve months' hard labour) and the following month, of onions (six months' hard labour for the instigator and three months' hard labour for each of the three accomplices).[61]

In April 1850 Constable 115, Jonas, described at Castle Hedingham Petty Sessions how, after being told of an alleged offence by John Thorogood, a Castle Hedingham baker, he'd examined a nearby ditch where traces of flour, alleged to have been stolen from Mr Thorogood's premises, had been found.

Having identified the footmarks of three people, he'd followed these to a fence, adjoining a local lane, where he'd found a button which he later matched with those on the coat of one of the three men he subsequently arrested on suspicion of the theft. Later that day, presumably acting on information from colleagues, Constable Jonas had apprehended the first suspect, who claimed to have been in bed at the time of the alleged theft. However, flour and dirt had been found on his clothes, and his shoes seemed likely to have made one of the sets of marks found by the ditch.

A second suspect had been arrested the same day, after flour and mud had been found on his clothes, and the following day the third suspect, whose button was missing and who also had mud and flour on his clothes, had been apprehended. Meanwhile the footmarks by the ditch had been examined by a local shoe maker who'd confirmed a correspondence with the shoes of the first suspect.[62] After evidence from a lodging house keeper, and local Constables Hart and Riddle, regarding movements of the suspects on the night of the alleged robbery, all three were found guilty, with sentences of nine months' hard labour for one, who had a previous conviction, and six months' each for the other two.[63]

Promotion of a Constable from 3rd to 1st class, which was essentially at the discretion of the Divisional Superintendent, could be relatively rapid.[64] However John waited six and a half years after becoming a Constable 2nd class before he was promoted, on 1 June 1851.[65]

Later that month, Constable 1st class Jonas was sent to Alphamstone, around 7 miles east of Castle Hedingham, to assist with an overnight observation, after an attempted burglary the previous month, on the home of a farmer, Edmund Cook.

While Constables Eldred (stationed at Bulmer) and Humphries (Lamarsh) remained outside, John waited in the house. Using an 'iron' bar, the burglars tried to enter at several places, before finally breaking through a kitchen window. One of them (Dawson), on being stopped by Constable Jonas, hit him on the head with the 'iron' bar before John retaliated with his baton and managed to pull Dawson to the floor and handcuff one of his wrists.

John Flower, a labourer employed by farmer Cook, attacked the other robber who'd entered (Poole) and for some minutes the two were locked in a fight during which Flower called for farmer Cook, who rushed to assist, with a loaded gun. However, Poole seized the gun, which was fired in the ensuing struggle, unfortunately hitting one of Flower's arms. Poole then struck farmer Cook with the gun before using it to beat Constable Jonas over the head and shoulders until he released Dawson, who concurrently seized Jonas's baton. Unarmed, Jonas repeatedly punched Dawson while Poole, who'd been slammed against the front door by Jonas, attacked Flower before turning to hit Jonas's head with a blow which stunned him. After this, Dawson and Poole made their escape with Pryke, a third burglar who was outside. Constable Humphries chased after Pryke but eventually lost him. Constable Eldred, who'd been climbing through the kitchen window when the gun was fired, also attempted to follow the fleeing Pryke but lost him, after falling over.

As the police had an idea of who the suspects were (in one report it was stated that they'd been identified, while in another it was claimed that they'd been informed on) and where they might be found, Constable Cross from Sudbury police station was contacted, and he soon arrested them in, or close to the town.

Medical aid was also sought from Sudbury, but amputation of John Flower's arm was unavoidable.

After initial custody in Sudbury gaol, the prisoners were taken to Castle Hedingham police station as the offence had occurred in Essex. While Pryke and Dawson awaited trial, Poole, who'd suffered a significant head injury, died, despite medical attention.[66]

Constable Jonas was too badly injured to attend the first committal hearing for Dawson and Pryke but had obviously recovered sufficiently to provide extensive evidence on the next occasion.

John's exertions and injuries were recognised in July in the form of a letter, from farmer Cook to the *Essex Standard*, praising his conduct, and the following month the newspaper reported that he and Constables Eldred and Humphries had been rewarded for their efforts.[67]

At the Summer Assizes in Chelmsford the charges against Dawson and Pryke were burglary and wounding with intent to murder (Constable Jonas).

Pryke was found not guilty of intent to murder but, despite being only the lookout, was sentenced to ten years' transportation.[68] Dawson pleaded guilty to both charges and, after narrowly avoiding the death penalty, was sentenced to transportation for life.[69]

However, such incidents weren't typical and life as a Constable in rural Essex soon returned to 'normal' with the 'usual' offences, such as theft by a labourer from the farm where he worked (six months' hard labour), in March 1852.[70]

John Jonas was promoted to Inspector (Insp.) 3rd Class on 1 January 1853, although he wasn't 'removed' from Sible Hedingham.[71] However, in May, he was relocated to Southminster, around 16 miles east, south-east of Chelmsford, at the eastern end of the Dengie peninsula.[72]

This location would have meant a time consuming, and probably costly, journey for the Jonas's.

Before railways made them redundant, coaches were used by a prosperous minority to travel between the main towns and cities, but the majority, and those wanting to travel to and from minor destinations, relied on 'carriers' who, using horses and carts, primarily moved goods around the country.[73]

Carriers continued to provide this service in areas without rail connections so probably not for the first time, and maybe not for the last, the Jonas's would have found themselves, together with all of their belongings and chattels, on a cart, on this occasion heading for Halstead, where they'd probably have had to arrange another carrier to take them to Chelmsford. If they were fortunate they then might have been able to arrange conveyance directly to Southminster but otherwise probably would have had to travel via, and hire the services of another carrier in, Maldon and/or Latchingdon.

Visits to Lavenham, around 50 miles north via Maldon, would, in the future, involve more than a few hours walk.

Getting to Southminster however was only one of the issues they faced, as the older children would have had to find jobs, and opportunities in the area may have been more limited than in the Colne Valley.

However, although this might have made the relocation even more difficult for the family, John probably welcomed the move. After spending his first four months as an Inspector in close proximity to his Superintendent, he would finally be in his own sub division, or district, and able to take on the full duties of his new rank. There may also have been some compensation for the rest of the family as, although the population was smaller than Lavenham, at least the town was largely self-contained, possibly because of its relative isolation.[74]

The Division extended from the parish of Woodham Walter in the north-west to that of Burnham in the south-east and from Bradwell in the north-east to the parish of Stow Maries in the south-west.[75] A police station at Latchingdon in the more densely populated western half of the Division (named after the peninsula) was the location for the Superintendent and the Petty Sessions.[76]

In the past, Dengie had been the scene of considerable smuggling activity but since the formation of the Coastguard service, and changes to the Excise duty structure, this had been significantly reduced.[77] Unsurprisingly therefore smuggling didn't lead to any (reported) cases for Insp. Jonas, although he no doubt would have had regular involvement with any Coastguard staff located in Dengie.[78] He would also probably have had considerable involvement with the Inspector and Constables paid for by the Burnham Oyster Company.[79]

John didn't have a Constable stationed at Southminster but, in addition to a county funded officer at Burnham, was probably responsible for those at Bradwell, Steeple and Tillingham, and possibly Althorne.[80]

As Southminster was relatively central to these locations it wouldn't have been difficult for the Inspector to brief his men daily, and for there to be considerable 'conferencing' between officers, as the Chief Constable had anticipated.[81]

In the absence of any at Southminster, which meant him patrolling as one, and relatively few otherwise available, John would probably have had to regularly undertake at least some of the tasks he knew from his experience as a Constable. As an Inspector however he would also have had many other responsibilities. Details of offences would have had to be entered onto a charge sheet which had to be copied and forwarded to the Superintendent. John would have had to arrange for accused to be taken before magistrates as soon as possible, and to ensure that Constables attended court when required, which could be often as it was necessary for them to at least 'prove' (confirm the identity of) an accused.[82] The frequent written orders from the Chief Constable had to be copied and passed on to the Constables, who also had to be briefed on their 'guards', which included anything specific to watch for and where they were to meet patrolling colleagues, which included himself or the Superintendent.[83] John would probably also have pointed out specific areas of interest in the latest *Police Gazette*.[84] Finally, on behalf of the Superintendent, John probably acted as the local Inspector of Weights and Measures.[85]

John's uniform would probably not have been dissimilar to that of a Constable, although braiding may have been substituted for some of the embroidery on the 'coat' collar. In 1855, as part of a re-organisation of the Essex force, there were some alterations to the uniform and the 'coat' became double breasted with two rows of eight buttons and a half inch (13mm) of black braid around the collar (together with an embroidered crown).[86]

In June, it was reported that Insp. Jonas had apprehended three labourers on a charge of stealing wood at nearby Asheldham (one months' hard labour each) and he was mentioned in cases of theft, at Tillingham, in December 1853 (acquitted) and January 1854 (four months' hard labour).[87]

As the Constable who seems to have replaced the Inspector at Southminster (no doubt as part of the Chief Constable's programme to reduce the number of Inspectors) arrived there in July 1854, it's likely that John was 'removed' around that time.

In mid September Insp. Jonas was called to investigate a burglary at a house in Stansted (Mountfitchet), where he noted that an object about 2 inches (50mm) wide had probably been used to smash some window panes, and observed blood on the broken glass.[88] On apprehending a suspect, John noticed two scratches and blood on her hand. The woman claimed that this was a three day old injury, but John suggested that it appeared more recent, leading the suspect to deny any knowledge of how the injury had been caused. On searching the suspect's house, John found a heavy bar which he compared with the marks left on a chest forced open during the burglary leading him to conclude that the bar had caused the marks. However, the suspected burglar was acquitted at the following Quarter Sessions.

Slightly larger than Southminster, but smaller than Lavenham, Stansted (Mountfitchet) was in south-west Essex, around 3 miles north of Bishops Stortford in Hertfordshire.[89] At that time it essentially consisted of Chapel (Street), part of the road between London and Newmarket, and the equally important and possibly busier, (Stansted) Street a few hundred yards (metres) to the east.

These were connected by Chapel Hill, which followed a gentle downward slope from the former to the latter, close to the southern end of which, in the valley of a minor tributary of the River Stort, was a station on the London - Cambridge railway line.[90]

Again the family had been uprooted and would have had to re-establish jobs and friendships; Lavenham, more than 35 miles north-east, remained more than a few hours walk.

By the time they reached Stansted, only Julia, who would then have been 7, was probably likely to be an attendee at one of the two schools in the town. Eleanor, probably 17, John (George), probably 16, and Alfred 14, would again have had to find work. In the case of Eleanor this might have been from home, possibly straw platting or dress making, or she may have found a job in a shop. This could be how she came into contact with George Phillips, her future husband, who she'd assist in running a bakery and grocery business.

It's probably reasonable to assume that John (George) and Alfred found what work they could, although for the first time they would have been able to use the railway to access opportunities outside of their immediate locality.

Relocation may have provided an opportunity to take more extensive accommodation than the family might previously have been able to arrange although it seems that, at least initially, they lodged at the home of a local doctor.[91]

Stansted was at the southern end of the Walden police Division which extended to the parish of Great Chesterford in the north and from that of Chrishall in the west, to Ashdon in the east.[92]

Although a Petty Sessions was held in the largest town, Saffron Walden, as the latter had retained a Borough police force, the county Superintendent was based in Newport where, similarly to Halstead, after the prisoners had been transferred to Chelmsford, the Constabulary had taken over the 'House of Correction' for use as a police station.[93]

Like the majority of sub divisions in Essex at this time, Stansted didn't have a police station, although there may have been a lock up of some description.[94]

John's responsibilities as the Inspector at Stansted would have been similar to those he'd undertaken at Southminster. He was probably in charge of Constables at Henham, Manuden and Stansted and, if they were divided reasonably equally with the other Inspector then in the Division, probably also at Clavering, Quendon and possibly Debden.[95] However, as Stansted was at the southern extremity of the district, daily briefings, in the way that they might have been managed at Southminster, may not have been possible so, as well as 'conferencing' at some central point, other arrangements may have been employed.

In January 1855, local Constable Wilkinson was informed by a Dr. Brook that money had disappeared from his home the previous evening. The doctor had been burgled repeatedly but hadn't been able to discover how entry had been made. Constable Wilkinson inspected the house and suggested that access might have been through the window of a room at the rear.

The following day, before going out, Dr. Brook carefully checked that all the doors were locked and that the window of the room at the rear was fastened, although he left the keys to a large wooden chest on the sideboard.

Also left in the house was Constable Wilkinson, who around 9 p.m. saw a William Ratcliff come to the window of the room at the rear. Ratcliff undid the fastening with a knife, opened the window and entered, before moving into the front room and opening a clock case. Constable Wilkinson then heard the rattle of keys and the large wooden chest being unlocked and locked. Ratcliff, holding several items, moved to the clock case before returning to the room at the rear where he was seized by Wilkinson, forced to the floor, and searched, although nothing stolen was found on him.[96]

As he'd apprehended Ratcliff, Constable Wilkinson had called out for Inspector Jonas, who was living in Dr. Brook's house at the time. Jonas quickly went to Wilkinson's assistance only to find that Ratcliff was already in custody, but on checking the keys left on the sideboard found that they'd been moved (four months' hard labour).[97]

Later in January Insp. Jonas apprehended a local labourer for stealing six chickens from a farm at Theydon Garnon, in the Epping Division (three months' hard labour).[98]

In June a man lodging at the Bell inn claimed that he'd been robbed of £20. Suspicion fell on another lodger who'd left the inn on the day of the robbery claiming that he was going to London. Inspector Jonas (presumably after asking questions at Stansted railway station ticket office) telegraphed the Superintendent at Wisbech, in Cambridgeshire, asking him to keep watch for the suspect.[99] When the Wisbech police later found the wanted man he was wearing a suit and a watch, which had cost £4 and £6 respectively. Two days later Insp. Jonas arrived (by train) to take possession of the offender, the items he'd bought, and the remaining £7 cash (six months' hard labour).[100]

In November 1855 Insp. Jonas found a sack of oats in the stable of a man suspected of being a 'receiver' of stolen goods. He later asked the man where the oats had come from and arrested him after an unsatisfactory response. Following that the Inspector arrested the man suspected of the theft, and he and the 'receiver' were sentenced respectively, to four and six months' imprisonment, with hard labour.[101]

The Inspector was involved in another case in the Epping Division, in April 1856, after he and his Superintendent had been deployed (possibly because they wouldn't be recognised locally) to observe activities at an Epping inn. Despite watching for at least two nights, and the Inspector discovering several 'trusses' of the hay alleged to have been stolen, the suspected thieves and 'receiver' were acquitted.[102]

# THE NORTH RIDING CONSTABULARY

In 1853 a (House of) Commons Select Committee (on Police) was established to consider the future of policing, particularly where a force hadn't already been formed. This eventually resulted in the 1856 County and Borough Police Act, which mandated all areas to have a full time, paid Constabulary (county) or Police (Borough) force. The first county to constitute a force under the Act was the North Riding (of Yorkshire), where the Constabulary was established on 14 October 1856.[103]

Many of the recommendations of the Commons Select Committee were based on the relatively extensive evidence provided by Captain (Capt.) McHardy, the Chief Constable of Essex, which some considered a 'model' for county forces.[104] It's not surprising therefore to find that one of the candidates for the post of North Riding Chief Constable, a Capt. Hill, had spent time in Essex, receiving guidance from Capt. McHardy.[105] Capt. Hill had probably been urged to do this by his eldest brother, John Richard Hill, a major landowner and influential magistrate, who it seems reasonable to believe had recognised the perceived leadership of Essex and the impact on his colleagues of one of his younger brothers having gained some first hand experience in the county.[106]

When it came to the vote for the post of Chief Constable, at the North Riding Quarter Sessions in mid October 1856, Capt. Hill was proposed by Lord Feversham, a powerful landowner and 'high profile' magistrate, who presented a 'reference' for Hill from Capt. McHardy.[107]

As Essex had a reputation for developing officers, which other counties had taken advantage of in the past, it would have been surprising if, while he'd been in the county, Capt. Hill hadn't identified any potential recruits to the Constabulary he soon might lead.[108] As he came from Thornton (Dale), his brother 'sat' (as a magistrate), usually at Pickering, and another brother, James, did the same at Kirkbymoorside or Helmsley, where Lord Feversham was also a member of the 'bench', it also seems probable that he would have been particularly watchful for a candidate for the Division which would cover those locations.[109]

In a statement made some years later, Capt. Hill related that the Essex Chief Constable had provided him with three officers (who presumably were seeking promotion) and it seems reasonable to believe that John was probably one of these.[110] He was relatively young but had significant experience, particularly in rural areas, with Borough forces (Saffron Walden and Sudbury) and probably with other counties (Hertfordshire).[111] It doesn't seem unreasonable to believe therefore that he might have been (conditionally) offered the post, he was soon to move to, by Capt. Hill, while the latter was in the county.[112]

Relocating over a distance as significant as that between Essex and the North Riding was relatively uncommon, but it wouldn't have been as difficult for the family as might initially be imagined, particularly as they'd probably become almost used to relocations and being more than walking distance from their families in Suffolk.[113]

Eldest daughter Eleanor (Ann) had recently married George Phillips in Stansted, and was no longer dependent, while John (George) and Alfred were entering adulthood and would probably also soon be independent.[114]

At the same time, the establishment of a large number of new forces, each requiring officers at all levels, was creating a unique opportunity, and, having possibly been held back for years, John may have been concerned that he might miss out in the future if he remained in Essex. Added to this was an always welcome increase in salary, so he (and Eleanor) probably felt that they had little choice.[115]

It's possible that they visited the area which Capt. Hill had probably discussed with John, but it seems unlikely. On a practical level it would have involved time, which John wouldn't normally have available, and money, which they might not have and/or wouldn't want to spend unnecessarily. If they remained in Essex, the chances were that they'd be given no choice anyway regarding future postings and be 'removed' to somewhere they didn't know. If, as was probable, they wouldn't be close to Lavenham, they might have considered that an unknown location in Yorkshire was little different from one in Essex. Finally, Capt. Hill is likely to have described his 'home' area in very positive terms – so was there any need to see for themselves, particularly as they might not be there for long?

We can imagine therefore that by the end of October, when the appointment of Capt. Hill had received Home Office approval and he'd been sworn in, that John would have begun putting his affairs in order.[116]

As there was no inter-force transfer mechanism at the time, this included his resignation from the Essex Constabulary, with effect from 30 November 1856. During his 14 years and 8 months' service the force had doubled in strength to around 200, two supervisory tiers had been introduced, in the form of Inspectors and Serjeants [*sic*], and an effective network of police premises had begun to be established.

## PICKERING LYTHE

John formally started with the North Riding Constabulary, as a Superintendent, at Pickering, on 1st December 1856.[117]

The ancient market town was the head-quarters of one of the new Constabulary's eight police Divisions which, according to the 1856 Act, were to be based on the historic Petty Sessional Divisions.[118] In the North Riding these were centred around the Wapentakes, which were similar to the Hundreds in other counties (such as Essex), although in practice, again as in Essex, there wasn't always a 'direct' match.

The Wapentake of Pickering Lythe, to give it the full title, included Scarborough, but that town, like Middlesbrough and Richmond, maintained a Borough force and wasn't, at this time, going to be absorbed into the North Riding Constabulary.[119] Possibly to compensate for this 'omission', the northern part of the Ryedale (or Rydale) Wapentake was included in the Pickering Division. This was slightly surprising, given that the Malton Division, which was to contain the remainder of the Ryedale Wapentake, was to be the least populated in the county.

However, the northern section had traditionally been 'independent' and as a separate Petty Sessional Division had maintained its own lock ups and Petty Sessions at Kirkbymoorside and also at Helmsley.[120] At the same time Pickering, was not only very similar in nature, with many shared interests, but also closely connected by a key 'main' road.

The Division therefore extended from the parishes of Helmsley and Oswaldkirk in the west, to those of Scalby and Cayton in the east.[121] The parish of Hackness, which was part of the Whitby Strand Wapentake, formed an incursion immediately west of Scalby, but was also to be policed as part of the Pickering Lythe Division.[122] The boundaries of the parish of Pickering, which extended around 20 miles from the Marishes in the south, to Goathland in the north, effectively formed the southerly and northerly extremities of the Division.

In a similar pattern of distribution found elsewhere in the Division, around three quarters of the population of the parish lived in the town of Pickering.[123] Situated on the southerly edge of the North York Moors it would have been a focal point for the limited numbers which managed to exist in the sometimes inhospitable and 'challenging' environment which they could present. It would also have been a focal point, although obviously for different reasons, for the greater numbers living in the area to the south of the east – west edge of the Moors. That was benign by comparison with the latter, and being fairly level and 'intensively' farmed wouldn't have seemed dissimilar to the parts of Essex and Suffolk that the Jonas's were most familiar with.

As well as being the largest town for some distance, Pickering was the natural centre of the Division as it not only lay on the road between Scarborough, around 16 miles east, via Kirkbymoorside and Helmsley, to Thirsk, but was also on the road from Malton, around 9 miles south, to Whitby. These 'main' roads however were very different to those we know today, which have often been straightened and widened, and directed away from villages such as Sinnington, and towns such as Kirkbymoorside.

Where possible, modern roads also remain on the level, rather than taking higher routes to avoid soft ground and/or areas regularly affected by flooding.

However, the 'main' roads were at least supposedly well maintained, which was less likely elsewhere. In 1856, for example, the number and size of holes on the road between Cropton and Hartoft Bridges attracted particular criticism, although other stretches elsewhere on the same route were considered to be probably as bad, if not worse.[124] Suggesting that this not only reflected the usual state of local roads, but also a continuing failure to maintain them, in 1869 a Cropton farmer offered to give up some of his land so that the road between Cropton and Wrelton could be improved.[125]

The state of the roads would have meant that travelling was time consuming (and probably very tiring), particularly if the route was uphill and/or involved conditions similar to those mentioned above. Visiting anywhere on the moors, or on their edge, such as Lastingham or Hutton (le Hole), must have been 'challenging'. Even with a horse, care would have had to be taken so that the animal didn't sustain an injury, or at least lose a shoe.

In response, local travellers probably used the most direct routes available, taking footpaths, tracks and the most minor roads.[126] For the police, difficulties in using the roads would probably be compensated by easier conversation with travellers, which was particularly important in collecting local intelligence, intercepting vagrants and pursuing alleged offenders.

Often the weather could further exacerbate the difficulties involved in moving around the area.

As well as being generally colder than East Anglia, the height of the moors meant that snow was far more common (and from as early as October until as late as June) and much deeper, often making them impassable for days or even weeks.[127]

Above average rainfall, which high lying areas attract, and/or thawing snow and ice, regularly resulted in the lower districts being flooded, and Pickering Beck and other local rivers, such as the Derwent and the Rye, regularly created their own impassable landscapes.[128] It isn't surprising that local news reports seem to have featured the weather as, or more often than any other issue.

When the roads were open, Pickering was the centre of considerable economic activity with a post office and two banks; and a market, on Mondays, which supplemented the many shops. The railway station, with regular services between Whitby and Rillington (around four miles east of Malton) was another key attraction of the town, as were regular livestock sales.

Once he'd managed to finish in Essex, John and the family faced the challenge of another relocation. Although they may have had little in terms of personal possessions, or domestic chattels to move, the journey alone would have been arduous.[129]

Several different railway companies were involved and, even when they could run over other company's lines, changing trains was inevitable. At that time there was no direct route between Doncaster and York and at the latter trains had to perform what must have been time consuming manoeuvres, considerably adding to the duration of many journeys.[130]

After what was probably a long and exhausting day it would have been dark when they disembarked in Pickering and, with few lights to illuminate the streets, they probably saw little of the area as they made their way to their accommodation.[131]

The following morning however they would probably have been pleasantly surprised as they discovered that the town had some similarities with Halstead - a wide main street, Market Place, sloping gently uphill from a river, Pickering Beck, to the parish church.[132]

Burgate and Willergate (Willowgate) ran off Market Place, while the shorter Bridge Street, Potter Hill and Train Lane lay west of the railway line. Bakehouse Lane (later Park Street) ran north from the western end of Market Place. To the south of the church was what became known as Smiddy (Smithy) Hill.

There was also significant development along the relatively level east - west 'main' road, designated locally as Eastgate, Hungate or Westgate, and for short distances off that, along 'roads' including Kirkham and Malton Lanes.

As with many of the small towns they'd lived in previously, Pickering was relatively self-contained. As well as several inns there were the usual shops and services: Baker, Barber, Boot Maker, Brewer, Butcher, Chemist, Clog Maker, Confectioner, Doctor, Draper, Dressmaker, Fishmonger, Fruit Dealer, Grocer, Hair Dresser, Ironmonger, Milliner, Milk Seller, Provisions Dealer, Solicitor, Tailor, Tallow Chandler, Tea Dealer, Watch Maker and Wine Merchant were among the many occupations listed in the 1861 Census.

Like many places, Pickering would have seemed familiar, although different, to what we see now. Some footpaths may eventually have been paved, and some of the busier roads surfaced, typically with stone setts or a mix of asphalt and stone, but otherwise both types of thoroughfare would probably have been no more than compressed earth.[133] However there would probably have been far less traffic, and of course none of it would have been motorised, although steam traction engines, often towing threshing machines, ploughing 'systems' or some other useful implements, would soon increasingly pass through.

As in every other town and village, the inns, shops and services would have been present in much greater numbers. Blacksmiths, farriers, saddlers, wheelwrights and other services related to horses would have been particularly evident, as would the waste that the latter left as they moved about. Women and (older) children may not have worked officially but many would have undertaken some local employment. Even if this was at home, women and children would have been regularly moving about their locality as water had to be fetched, waste disposed of and shops visited, probably daily. If not at school or employed in some way, children would be playing in the streets or local fields. Men would be walking to or from work, including at meal times. On Sundays many people went to some form of religious service and on Mondays most people would have visited the market(s).

At other times there were social events. The landed and wealthy minority engaged in hunting and shooting, while a larger minority attended band or choir practices, or concerts; bible classes or temperance meetings, dinners or balls, lectures or readings, recitals or plays; militia meetings or rifle practice.

Considerably more were drawn to agricultural or horticultural shows, cricket matches and later association football games; fairs, flower shows, foot races, hare coursing, horse races and horse shows.

Tourists would also have been an increasingly familiar sight, particularly as the railway network developed, and the considerable number of travellers, always to be found on the roads, probably took their time as they passed through the town, whether on foot, horseback, or in some sort of conveyance.[134]

So there would have been far more people (walking) on the streets and almost all of them would have been immediately accessible in a way that contemporary travellers seldom are.

Pickering lock up, which was to become the Jonas's new home, was on 'lower' Hallgarth, looking across Hungate and the bottom of Smithy (Smiddy) Hill (which led west past the Cattle Market to Birdgate and Market Place).[135] With three cells at the rear and probably a charge room and possibly some other official accommodation at the front, John and the family presumably occupied, for a rent likely to have been around 4 – 5s (20 – 25p) per week, the upper two of the three floor, stone, building.[136] The family may have had a living and a dining room, separate kitchen and several bedrooms.[137] It's likely that there would have been a 'privy' although as in previous locations there wouldn't have been any modern facilities.[138]

There'd been a works in the town since 1847, but gas was only to become generally available around 20 years later, which meant that they not only would have continued with a coal or wood fuelled range for cooking, but also probably with 'oil' or candles for lighting.[139]

As the building, part of a continuous row of houses and cottages, was effectively on the east – west, and close to the south – north, 'main' roads through the town (and close to the centre) it was in a prominent location. However, their Suffolk accent and possibly at least some of them being above average height might have made the family noticeable anyway.[140] At the same time, John's role, and their relationship with him, meant that they would always, to some extent, also be distanced from the rest of the community.[141]

With the ground floor of the building continuing in the role of lock up - prisoners were recorded there in the 1871 Census - for the first time in his career Supt. Jonas had full responsibility for a police station. Although this might have meant that effectively he'd never be off duty, that may not have led to a substantive change in the lives of John or his family.[142] It also wouldn't have been unusual, as in a rural area such as Pickering, many people worked every day of the week and every week of the year as, at the very least, animals had to be fed and watered.[143] Otherwise in a town, 8 a.m. – 7 p.m. with at least 8 a.m. – 1 p.m. on Saturdays, was considered usual.[144] Early closing of shops, and days off, other than Sundays, were so infrequent as to warrant mention in the local press.[145]

As well as moving himself, and his family, John had several other issues to contend with before he could properly begin his new role.[146]

One the most critical matters facing John may have been a Superintendent Constable. John Heselhurst, who the *Cleveland General Association* had employed as a policeman at Stokesley, between 1839 and 1842, was resident in the lock up on Hallgarth in 1851.[147]

He may have been there when the North Riding Constabulary was being formed, as the *York Herald* reported his involvement, as the superintendent policeman [*sic*], in a case in Pickering, in August 1856. If he was still living at the police station to be, when the Jonas's arrived in Pickering, the situation would have been at least difficult, as they may have been forced to make temporary accommodation arrangements.[148]

Besides the Heselhurst issue, John would have had the tasks of helping the family to adjust to yet another upheaval, and (eventually) settling into their new home. John (George) and Alfred would have had to find jobs and Julia, by then 9, enrolled into a new school.[149]

In regard to his position, Supt. Jonas would also have had to ensure that everything expected by the Chief Constable was acquired and/or arranged, including a uniform for himself, if that hadn't already been provided.

As the same company supplied both forces, this may have been similar to, or the same as, an Essex Superintendent, consisting of 'dress' trousers, tall hat and a blue 'frock coat' with two rows of silver buttons, silver braid around the cuffs and black braid on the collar.[150] John would have supplied his own boots (winter) and shoes (summer), for which he got an allowance, as these were part of the issue in Normanby's *Rules*.

The Chief Constable interviewed and appointed every new entrant who then spent an initial three or four weeks at Northallerton.[151] Sometime during, but probably at the end of that period, uniforms and essential items, such as batons, handcuffs and whistles (rather than rattles) may have been issued.[152]

From January 1857 new entrants were also issued with the North Riding *Orders and ...* which provided the same type of guidance and parameters which had probably helped John when he'd been a new Constable.[153]

The Superintendent soon had his Establishment filled, with Inspectors at Kirkbymoorside and East Ayton (usually referred to as Ayton) and Constables at the former, Cayton, Great Barugh, Helmsley, Pickering (two), Oswaldkirk, Thornton (Dale), Scalby, Snainton and Wrelton.[154] These stations however weren't necessarily permanent, as from time to time Constables moved between them and to/from other locations, presumably as local needs dictated and/or the availability of accommodation changed.[155]

As well as dealing with any induction issues which his recruits might have been experiencing, Supt. Jonas may also have had to help when they'd moved location, and/or when they'd taken over other existing law enforcement related accommodation, such as at Helmsley and Kirkbymoorside.[156]

Early debates at the Quarter Sessions had led to a proposal for a force of no more than 90, including the Chief Constable and Superintendents, but eventually the number agreed was 50.[157] However, after the swearing in of Capt. Hill, he was directed to examine the requirements, bearing in mind the number agreed initially and the population of the Riding being 188,755.[158] This led to a consensus for a force of 100, although that remained considerably less than the government permitted maximum. However the number increased over time as the Chief Constable's reports to almost every succeeding Quarter Sessions included the need for additional manpower (and/or buildings).[159]

Initially such increases didn't benefit the Pickering Lythe Division. The second Constable in Pickering was withdrawn from July 1857, although from November, after when it remained unaltered for some time, the original Establishment number was reinstated, when a Constable was stationed at Hutton le Hole.

As in Essex, a horse and two wheeled cart, or trap, was allocated to each Divisional head-quarters, although it seems that in the North Riding horses and carts were also provided to other officers.[160] The cart was to be employed if someone, usually a prisoner, had to be conveyed but otherwise officers used only the horse, or walked.[161]

# CONSTABULARY DUTIES

Although a Superintendent, in such a rural area, with relatively few officers, when time allowed and/or circumstances necessitated, John seemed to have shared in the work of his Constables, in the same way as his Inspectors.[162] Until some local support was provided, several years later, John would also have had to undertake those duties of a local Inspector, or Sergeant, in regard to the Constables in his district, which, as well as at Pickering, were those at Great Barugh, Thornton (Dale) and Wrelton; and later Lockton. Among other tasks, this would have included briefings, agreeing 'conference' points, and arranging 'coverage' of Pickering police station, or at least of any prisoners awaiting trial or transport elsewhere.[163]

The Superintendent was also required to visit each 'township' in his district at least once a month, meet his Constables at 'conference' points and would have had to liaise regularly with his Inspectors (and Sergeants).[164]

One of John's most significant responsibilities would have been in regard to Pickering Petty Sessions.[165] As well as attending to 'charge' any accused that he'd personally arrested, and to 'prove' the identity of an accused, the Superintendent had a key role in the operation of the court.

Prior to the 'new' police, most prosecutions for criminal offences had been by private individuals and this practice continued well into the second half of the century, although the police increasingly took over the responsibility.

This meant that the Superintendent acted as the prosecutor, so (newspaper) reports mention that John called witnesses and cross examined accused.[166] This role became more important as the simplification of the penal system, earlier in the century (and lately the 1855 Criminal Justice Act), meant that an increasing number of cases were tried by the local magistrates rather than being sent to the Quarter Sessions or Assizes.[167]

Pickering Petty Sessions primarily used the Black Swan in Birdgate, or the White Swan on Market Place, but from January 1861 began using an upper room in a new building at the eastern end of Market Place, which was also used for a savings bank and as a news room/literary institute.[168]

As well as, but in connection with Petty Sessions, some of John's other responsibilities would have included making himself aware of new legislation and maintaining an understanding of the law and legal proceedings (and briefing his officers in this regard); and making annual returns to the magistrates summarising the previous year's crimes and the operation of the licensing laws.[169]

John would have had to be particularly conversant with Articles 6, 7 and 8 in *Orders and ...* , which were specifically for Superintendents and included the monthly, quarterly and annual returns required by the Chief Constable.[170] Occasionally, serious crimes had to be investigated, and colleagues, including from outside the Division, had to be assisted with the apprehension of offenders.[171]

The Superintendent additionally had several non police roles, including again acting as the local Inspector of Weights and Measures.[172]

He had to inspect the state of the roads and, when their condition was unsatisfactory, prosecute those responsible for maintaining them (in a similar vein he may also have acted as an inspector of nuisances).[173]

In addition, he probably undertook the role of assistant Relieving Officer for vagrants (for the Pickering Poor Law Union) and, possibly not unconnected with that position, acted as an inspector of lodging houses.[174]

John would also have had a role managing the visits of the Inspector of Constabulary, as the latter aimed to check every police station, charge room, cell or lock up, and every officer.[175]

However, while the range of Superintendent's responsibilities may seem onerous, particularly when combined with ongoing issues and everyday events/incidents, the time involved in addressing them was probably highly variable. On the other hand, it isn't difficult to understand how John might have used at least some of the time which would have resulted from being on duty almost all day, and the best part of every evening.

As in rural Essex, John's team in Pickering Lythe were primarily concerned with petty crime.[176] The vast majority of the reported cases at Pickering were assault, with drink related offences almost as common. It was much the same in the eastern and western districts of the Division, although reports of poaching and vagrancy seem to have been more prevalent in the former. In addition, there were cases of broken (labour) contracts, domestic disputes, animal cruelty, obstructing the highway, dangerous driving of carriages, carts or wagons; and failure to pay rates or support for a family or family member.[177]

Burglary was not a common crime, probably as few had anything of value in their homes, but it was an issue for those perceived as being worth burgling, with some repeatedly targeted.[178] Theft was also generally not common, but watches were probably the exception as they were easily concealed about the person and could be readily disposed of at a pawnbroker's or second hand shop. Generally infrequent (but demonstrating that these are not contemporary phenomena) there were also sexually related incidents, which included what was almost certainly rape, or attempted rape, although not referred to as that.[179] However, harassment of young women by groups of young men, particularly in towns, was common.

Despite the potential workload, the Coroner at an 1872 Inquest was to state that the North Riding was relatively free of crime, a contention generally supported by the Chief Constable's reports to the Quarter Sessions.[180]

# MISADVENTURE

In October 1857, only months after beginning with the new force, John was promoted to Superintendent 1 $^{st}$ Class. However, events were soon to question his appointment.

Less than a year later, in June 1858, the *Malton Messenger* reported that a policeman had gone into the George, on Market Place in Pickering, and struck someone with his baton. The victim had laid unconscious for some time and there'd been fears for his life.

The omission of the policeman's name from the report, when in a relatively small town such as Pickering it's likely that he would have been well known, seems unusual, and it's not unreasonable to believe that it may have been Supt. Jonas.[181]

In August, the *York Herald* reported that magistrates had been appointed to investigate an accusation that Supt. Jonas had engaged in a horse race with a local man, and encouraged him to visit public houses. The report continued that, as the magistrates had established the charges against him, Supt. Jonas had been suspended from his post and moved to Castle Howard as a Constable.[182]

The newspaper added that Supt. Jonas had contended that he was riding casually when the local man made a flattering remark in regard to the potential of his horse, leading them to try each other's mounts. John had also claimed that they'd only trotted for about 150 yards (140m), only visited two public houses and only had a single drink at each.[183]

John may not have intended to engage in anything more than 'banter' and these 'offences' may seem minor, but that was far from the case.

Generally police officers' behaviour was not only to be beyond reproach but specifically *Orders and* ... forbade officers from entering public houses, except on duty.[184] In this instance John had not only disobeyed that instruction, but as the officer ultimately responsible for prosecuting drunken behaviour, and for controlling licensed premises, had done much worse as he'd not only indulged in, but was believed to have encouraged the consumption of alcohol.[185] If, in addition, he'd also engaged in any form of race, he'd broken other *Orders and* ... instructions which forbade driving county horses faster than 6 mph and using them for purposes other than public service.[186]

However, while John may have been guilty of several transgressions, the potential source of the story and the nature of the newspaper coverage suggest that this incident may have had some hidden overtones.

The licensees of the establishments visited, or people connected to them, may have made an issue of the episode for political reasons. However, a more likely source for the initial report, and one that would have probably carried more weight with the local magistrates, was the other man who was involved. His father was a local farmer who may 'in passing' have simply related his son's story to his neighbours, innocently leading to the involvement of the magistrates. On the other hand, he may have been one of many in the country who had been, and possibly continued to be, against the concept (and cost) of the 'new' police forces.

If that was the case, the farmer would no doubt have taken some satisfaction in telling his neighbours, one of whom was a senior member of the Pickering 'bench', that they had a Superintendent who considered himself equal in some way to a man of property (the son later inherited his father's considerable land holding). At a time when deference to anybody with some degree of status seems to have been almost mandatory, this alone would have magnified the seriousness of any offence in the opinion of many. However even if that hadn't been the case, as the incident involved someone who it seems he had probably specifically selected for this posting, it would have been particularly embarrassing for the Chief Constable.

It's this which might have led to the reported involvement of the magistrates in the case, if that wasn't otherwise a result of the newspaper misunderstanding, or being misinformed.[187]

Although they wielded significant influence, one of the developments which had accompanied the creation of the 'new' police was that magistrates no longer had any direct control over them. It was for the Chief Constable, not the magistrates, to investigate accusations against his officers, determine their guilt (or otherwise) and decide on the appropriate action.

However in this case, due to the particular location and individuals, Capt. Hill may have allowed, or even have asked, the magistrates to become involved, not least perhaps so that he could be seen to be impartial. Alternatively, his (elder) brother might have exerted pressure for him, and his other brother and colleagues, to be allowed to dispense 'local justice'.

This may have been simply to enable them to demonstrate to the community that they retained the same sort of influence that they'd always had (before the creation of the Constabulary).

Another possibility is that other issues were behind the magistrates' involvement and that the incident in the George and the episode on the Malton road were linked in some way.[188] The latter may have been designed to remove John and/or to make the magistrates' influence and power clear to him (and to others).

Despite what, if anything, may have been behind the incident and despite why, and if, the magistrates were involved, and in the way that the newspaper reported, in what may have been a highly embellished story, there is no way of knowing what effect that had on the final outcome of the case.

This was the 'de-ranking' and (consequent) removal of John.[189]

Although not necessarily conclusive, police records only mention drunkenness in regard to John, and unless he was trying to hide something, there is no reason why the Chief Constable wouldn't have recorded any other offence he (rather than the magistrates) considered pertinent.

On the other hand, while cases can never be directly comparable, a Superintendent found guilty of drunkenness in June 1861 was only 'de-ranked' to Inspector, which suggests that John was (considered to be) guilty of much more than simply that offence. If that was the case it may have been only the nature of his appointment, and him seemingly being the first senior officer to have offended, which saved John from dismissal.

It also makes the adjudication of Capt. Hill, who had to be seen to sanction behaviour which was considered inappropriate, seem not unreasonable. However, 'de-ranking' to Constable may have been considered worse than dismissal, as the loss of status would have been unacceptably humiliating to many. On the other hand, that may have been exactly what the magistrates wanted and was likely to have set an example for others.

Perhaps if John accepted his punishment, demonstrated that he'd 'learnt his lesson' and reacted positively, not everything he'd achieved in his career so far would be lost. His new 'station' at Welburn was one of only three in the Malton Division.[190]

Similar in size, if not in nature to Foxearth, the village wasn't too far from Pickering and with a post office, schools (Julia was probably still an attendee) and a station, Castle Howard on the line between York and Malton, there were at least some of the facilities that the family were used to.

However, employment opportunities living in Welburn may have been limited for John (George) and Alfred, even if they'd travelled to work, so it seems probable that this may have been when they moved away, possibly to Middlesbrough, where they were working as joiners at the time of the 1861 Census.[191]

The family therefore not only lost their home but were probably separated as a result of John's misadventure(s).

However, after what seems a relatively short period of time, particularly for a 'disgraced' officer, in late July 1859 Constable 47, Jonas, was promoted to Sergeant in the Langbaurgh Division.[192]

63

Although he might have been of exceptional assistance to the Superintendent he'd reported to directly, in nearby Malton, this seems unusual as there was unlikely to have been anything in a year of 'normal' activities in a 'quiet' rural station to warrant the promotion of a Constable. However, it may not only have been the first stage in a 'rehabilitation' of John, but may also have resolved a recruitment difficulty.

Whatever was the case, and it may have been a combination of both, John was to occupy a rank which he would otherwise have missed and in, what for him, was probably a novel environment.

In September, Sergeant Jonas moved to South Stockton.[193]

Yet again the family was going to face the upheaval of a relocation, but at least the township offered the same, if not more, facilities than Welburn. In addition, as South Stockton and Middlesbrough were only separated by a short railway journey, or a walk of around a couple of hours, John and Eleanor (and Julia) would at least have been able to see John (George) and Alfred more regularly and more easily.

Typical offences in South Stockton seem to have been drunkenness, minor assault, desertion of employer, minor theft and desertion of family. While the relatively low number of (newspaper) reports of such crimes don't seem to warrant the Establishment which Sergeant Jonas was part of, the Chief Constable had for some time been expressing concern over a surge in population, and the need for a lock up in the town.[194] In addition the proximity of rapidly developing areas such as Middlesbrough, and the main conurbation of Stockton, had the potential to add to the police workload at any time.[195]

Outside of South Stockton, Sergeant Jonas and his two, later three, Constables were responsible for policing Thornaby (also served by South Stockton railway station), which was gradually merging with its northern neighbour. To the south of Thornaby was a relatively large rural area, where the next police station was Yarm, while to the east the nearest stations were at North Ormesby and Marton.

In early September 1860, after what again seems a relatively short period of time, the *York Herald* reported that John had been re-appointed as Superintendent at Pickering, after his replacement had been dismissed.[196]

Removal from Pickering, and the post of Superintendent, for only a little over two years (and after dismissal had been avoided) might suggest that the Chief Constable had significant confidence in John's ability. Alternatively, it might indicate that he didn't want to appear to have made a poor choice in his original appointment.

Another possibility may be, if there was any more to the incident on the Malton road than had been reported by the *York Herald*, that the Chief Constable might have been anxious to bring a close to the episode.

Whatever had led to their absence, and might have occurred during that period, John (and Eleanor) must have been hugely relieved to return to Pickering, although this may have been tempered by the absence of John (George) and Alfred.

However, in April 1862 John (George) joined the North Riding Constabulary which he and the family might have hoped would present an opportunity for him to work, and live, closer to them.[197]

This change may have been the catalyst for Alfred to relocate and it seems likely to have been when he moved to Rosedale, some 12 miles north-west of Pickering.[198] This would have meant him being able to make regular visits to the latter, which may be how he renewed a friendship with, or met, a Margaret Lawson, who lived with her grandmother, Rachel, three 'up' Hallgarth from his parents.[199]

## NEW START

Little changed in the Division after John was 'removed', and the role he returned to was essentially the same as that he'd been moved away from, just over two years earlier. However, some new issues were developing as others continued.

One of the latter was vagrancy. In one week in October 1861, for example, the *Malton Messenger* reported that a tramp who'd been lodging in Eastgate was wanted for theft (and had been pursued to Malton, Scarborough and Whitby among other places); a man had been arrested in Aislaby for hawking without a licence (three weeks' hard labour at Northallerton); and at Wilton a woman had been arrested for stealing (three weeks' at Northallerton for vagrancy).[200] In addition, there were two separate cases of people, found sleeping in outbuildings, being sentenced to a months' hard labour at Northallerton.

In January 1867 Supt. Jonas traced two 'rangers' to Whitby, after they'd stolen various items from the quarry at Newbridge (three months' hard labour), and a year later, while investigating a burglary, arrested six men for sleeping unlawfully in a farm's outbuilding (one months' hard labour each).[201]

In the early hours of a morning, in September 1873, a tramp broke windows at Pickering railway station while drunk and extremely disorderly. His explanation, that he didn't know what he'd been doing, as he'd been drinking for five weeks, didn't prevent him from receiving twenty one days' hard labour.[202]

In March the following year, after being charged by Supt. Jonas with begging, a man with thirteen previous convictions at Pickering for the same offence, was sent to the Quarter Sessions. As the accused was known to travel around the Riding, as a professional beggar, he was gaoled for six months.[203]

A new issue for everyone in the force was the control of animal diseases. Cattle Plague, Pleuro Pneumonia, Foot & Mouth and Hydrophobia (Rabies) were all major causes for concern in the North Riding in the 1860s and 1870s.[204]

The Chief Constable seems to have issued his first directions regarding diseases in cattle and sheep in September 1862, and continued to generate instructions over the coming years.[205] In September 1865 he specifically mentioned Cattle Plague, and two months later the scale of the problem became evident to anybody who wasn't already aware, as Pickering livestock market was closed.[206]

In January 1866 Supt. Jonas prosecuted nine individuals, with moving cattle contrary to the Cattle Plague legislation.[207] A Lastingham man was fined 10s (50p) and he and the other eight had a total of £4 3s 6d (£4.17½) in costs levied, with the magistrates promising to be more severe if further cases appeared before them.[208]

Locally, Pleuro Pneumonia seems to have been as prevalent and as problematic as Cattle Plague, and was one of the subjects of Supt. Jonas's monthly reports to the magistrates for many years. In July 1871 the Superintendent charged a farmer in the Marishes with failing to report the disease, and as late as November 1875, reported an outbreak on another farm in the Marishes, which had led to an animal being destroyed.

The following June, Supt. Jonas shot a cow, the second to be destroyed in a month on the same farm, at the Hole of Horcum, Saltersgate, around 8 miles north of Pickering.[209]

Although it arrived later, and didn't have the same 'profile' as Cattle Plague or Pleuro Pneumonia, Foot & Mouth disease was also problematic during this period. In a single week in September 1869 Supt. Jonas reported 151 cases of Foot & Mouth in the towns and villages around Pickering.

In early 1870 the implications of the Contagious Diseases Act led the Quarter Sessions to agree that Divisional Superintendents should take on another non police role by acting as animal health inspectors, specifically in regard to Foot & Mouth disease.[210] The epidemic continued, and outbreaks were being reported as late as September 1875.

In May 1870, following deaths elsewhere in the country and several local cases of Hydrophobia, notices were fixed around the Division advising that the police would shoot any un-muzzled dog, and any unclaimed strays.[211]

While John had been away, in 1859, as the Constabulary took over that responsibility, an office for the adjustment of weights and measures had been provided at Hallgarth to enable the police to discharge their new duties.[212]

With the importance seemingly attached to this additional role, it isn't surprising that in May 1861 John, the local Inspector of Weights and Measures, prosecuted a rag merchant, miller, innkeeper and five grocers for various offences including unstamped measures, scales, weights and weighing machines; as well as 'light' or 'heavy' weights.[213] The offending items were 'seized' and fines of 6d (2½p) and costs were awarded in each case.

Having prosecuted a fish merchant, in July 1863, for selling food unfit for humans, in October that year John prosecuted a Middleton shop keeper for possessing unbalanced scales, a Pickering licensee for 'short' measures for pints, half pints, quarter pints and half quarter pints and a Thornton (Dale) shop keeper for having a 'short' (or 'light') weight.

Perhaps surprisingly, such prosecutions didn't seem to diminish. In November 1867, for example, John prosecuted several shopkeepers for wrongly balanced scales, and one for an inaccurate yard (metre) measure, while in 1873 he prosecuted another for 'light' weights.[214]

In August 1863, five years after the Local Government Act which enabled it, the town formed a Local Board to administer what had become a Local Government District.[215] The Board's responsibilities included providing sewers, supplying water, clearing 'nuisances' from, and cleaning the streets, although in the case of Pickering only the water supply and the metalling of streets and footpaths, seem to have attracted the attention of the local newspaper.

The formation of the Board (as it would be able to levy rates) may have generated the same type of opposition which the 'new' police forces had encountered. Opponents no doubt pointed to improvements which had already been made in the town, such as paving of the north side of Market Place in 1859 and the flagging of Eastgate, completed in early 1861, in the same way that before 1839 (and 1856) others had praised parish constables and watchmen.[216] There was also some suggestion that the Local Board may have been constituted to avoid the town being included in a Highways District, as required under the 1862 Highways Act, which was strongly opposed in the area.[217]

If that had been the case their efforts had been in vain as in December 1867 a Highways Board, covering Pickering, was established.[218] Although that may have reduced some of the Superintendent's workload regarding roads, just as the formation of the Local Board may have done in regard to nuisances, it didn't remove his responsibilities, which a case in March 1865 had illustrated.[219]

That month John summonsed the two Kirby Misperton highway surveyors for neglecting to maintain three hundred yards (270m) of road between Kirby Misperton and the bridge over Costa Beck, nine hundred yards (820m) leading to Great Habton and another four hundred yards (370m) in the direction of Little Barugh. The magistrates instructed that repairs were to be made within a fortnight and that Supt. Jonas was then to inspect the roads and report again on their condition. A fine of £3 was to be imposed if the works had not been carried out (satisfactorily).[220]

This wasn't a unique case however, as in November there was almost a repetition, involving Middleton Low Lane and the two Middleton highway surveyors.[221]

Supt. Jonas also supported travellers indirectly, through regular prosecutions for obstructing the highway. In May 1861 a local pig dealer paid 2s (10p) costs, after being charged by John with leaving animal manure on the footpath in Market Place.[222] A Pickering farmer was fined 8s (40p), in March 1865, for leaving a wagon and horses in the Cattle Market for more than two hours.[223] In June 1868, Supt. Jonas charged two masons from Pickering with obstructing the highway by playing 'pitch and toss'. Each was fined, and awarded costs of 8s 6d (42½p), with an alternative of fourteen days in prison.[224]

Roads were also an issue in other ways during this period. While the toll bars on the Malton – Scarborough and York – Malton roads were removed in September 1865, they were retained (until June 1870) on the road between Pickering and Malton.[225]

From an operational point of view this probably mattered little to Supt. Jonas as the police were able to pass without payment, and his responsibilities regarding the roads would probably have been unchanged. On the other hand, journeys between Pickering and Malton could be difficult, including for the police, as a dispute over the maintenance of the Howe Bridge section of the road continued, (eventually reaching the High Court).[226]

Despite that long standing issue and probable awareness of the Superintendent's responsibility in regard to roads, in January 1866 the toll collector at the Old Malton bar perhaps surprisingly demanded payment from John when, accompanied by Eleanor, he passed through.[227] The collector was summonsed for unlawfully demanding and taking a toll, when the police 'vehicle' shouldn't have been charged, and was fined 5s (25p) with 11s 6d (57½p) costs.[228]

In early 1871 the state of the town's paving and street lighting attracted strong criticism.[229] The paving issue may have been the reason, the following year, for the Board ordering 1,000 tons of stone, and instructing the surveyor to asphalt Eastgate, Park Street and Westgate, and later Burgate.[230] However the lighting situation didn't seem to have been improved, as in May 1872 the *York Herald* reported that the majority of the population wanted the streets to be lit until later in the evening, and for the lighting 'season' to be extended further into the summer period.[231]

On the other hand, the Board were becoming increasingly conscientious over other responsibilities, such as building control (demanding that houses had downpipes) and planning (reviewing applications for extensions and new buildings).[232] The Board also demonstrated what is now called environmental health awareness, as for example, they refused permission for a new tannery on the grounds that it would pollute the principal water supply for Bridge Street, Potter Hill and Train Lane. The medical inspector for the Board however continued to be dissatisfied with the condition of some of the town's water supply.

The need to manage various new responsibilities was probably one of the reasons for a gradual increase in Constabulary numbers in the Division during this period.

When John returned to Pickering the deployment pattern he'd left in August 1858 remained in place, continuing until November 1861, when a Constable joined the Inspector at Ayton.

By October 1862 a 'resident' Constable was stationed at Rosedale, after the Chief Constable told Quarter Sessions that he hoped that the post would be funded by the Rosedale Iron Company (probably in the type of arrangement, which John would have been familiar with, as that which had existed between the Essex Constabulary and the Burnham Oyster Company).[233] A Constable was stationed at Staintondale by November 1862, after Capt. Hill informed the same Quarter Sessions that, while they'd been travelling over what the *York Herald* described as the extensive and wild district between Whitby and Scarborough, Lt. (Lieutenant) Colonel Woodford, the Inspector of Constabulary who (then) covered the North Riding, had suggested the need for a Constable in that area.[234]

From January 1865 a Constable was stationed at Lockton and, following another request for an additional officer for Pickering Lythe West/Ryedale in August, a further Constable was located at Rosedale by September 1866, although that post was replaced by a Sergeant in December.

A Constable had provided a police presence at Falsgrave by March 1869 and during May the Constable at Ayton was replaced by a Sergeant.[235] Also in May, the Constable at head-quarters in Pickering was supplemented by a Sergeant or another Constable.[236] Following on from these deployments, a Constable was stationed at Ampleforth from January 1870, and in one of the changes occurring almost monthly, as four Sergeant's posts were added one by one to the Establishment, the post at Helmsley was converted to a Sergeant's from December 1871.[237]

Constabulary numbers in the Division therefore drifted upwards from thirteen or fourteen in 1857, to twenty two or twenty three by autumn 1872.[238]

This increase reflected a similar expansion of the overall North Riding force. According to the Inspector of Constabulary's annual reports, which were based on the Establishment at the end of September each year, in 1857 the force numbered 105, increasing to 123 in 1862, 153 in 1867 and 185 in 1872, although these numbers were increasingly swollen by privately funded officers. Despite the generally upward trend however even by 1872 the ratio with the population was only one to 1,388, which remained significantly below the permitted maximum.

A key issue for Supt. Jonas arising from the increase in numbers, and the complexity of the rank structure, would have been the need for increased communication.

Once the forces instituted under the 1856 Act became established, and those which had been formed through earlier Acts became used to being part of a national structure, they probably began to consider how they could be helped by (and could help) each other.

In the absence of a national system of criminal records and few, if any, local ones, this was critical, and why an interchange of information through the pages of the *Police Gazette* seems to have become of increasing importance.[239] In Pickering Lythe the *Gazette* was primarily used to seek information about burglaries and thefts; absconders and suspects; and increasingly frequently, after the 1869 Habitual Criminals and 1871 Prevention of Crimes Acts, to seek or share information.[240] Supt. Jonas's briefings would have become more essential, more extensive and possibly more frequent.

With the workload in the Pickering Lythe Division mounting, as reflected by the increases and/or changes in the Establishment, the opening of the railway connection between Malton and Helmsley, via Gilling, in October 1871 may have been the catalyst for a review of Divisional boundaries. The Malton Division had always been minor (in Establishment and size) by comparison with Pickering Lythe, and it isn't surprising, with the opening of the line between Helmsley and Kirkbymoorside overdue (finally occurring in January 1874), that the Ryedale district was re-allocated to Malton in February 1873.[241] This would not only have reduced the Pickering Lythe workload but also that of Supt. Jonas personally. A smaller Establishment meant less time on personnel related issues and a smaller area meant less time on events/incidents he might be required to assist with, administrative tasks and possibly some of the non police activities he had to undertake.

75

However, although the Pickering Lythe Establishment was reduced to around fourteen, that was more than the number that had been in post when the Division was formed, and numbers soon began to increase again anyway.

One reason for this and for the increase in numbers which had occurred over the years, was Rosedale.

Ironstone had begun to be commercially exploited in several locations on the moors in the 1850s, and operations had begun on the West side of Rosedale by 1857.[242] This was followed by activity on the East side in 1859, and after the mines were connected to the rail network in 1861 and 1865 respectively, output would rise to a peak of over 560,000 tons in 1873.[243]

Increasing production in the relatively isolated, and sometimes climatically inhospitable, location meant offering relatively high wages which attracted miners and other workers from as far as Ireland. By 1862 some 250 men were working in the dale and five years later, after the construction of the railways had temporarily added another 200 – 300, around double that number were employed.[244] This increased to almost 2,000 in 1870 (and was in excess of 3,000 in 1874).[245]

While the mining company attempted to ameliorate their impact, by for example building accommodation and providing social facilities, the typical problems associated with an itinerant and probably relatively young, male workforce, such as drunkenness, theft and violence, became increasingly common. The small hamlet of Rosedale Abbey, and the few farmers and their labourers who otherwise populated the valley, would have been overrun almost as soon as operations began.[246]

Officers weren't stationed at Rosedale when mining began, probably because of a shortage of accommodation and/or they weren't warranted, although in March 1858 two Constables at Kirkbymoorside were described as being on Special Duty, which may have been related. As noted above, Rosedale was provided with a Constable from October 1862, a second Constable from September 1866, and a Sergeant from December the same year. [247]

At the Lent Quarter Sessions in 1871, one of the senior Pickering magistrates stated that the 'difficult' circumstances in Rosedale led to 'prize' fights, drunkenness and a generally unsatisfactory situation, made worse by a lack of police facilities.[248] In June that year Supt. Jonas presented a petition from the inhabitants of Rosedale to the magistrates at Pickering, seeking an additional Constable to cope with the increasing size of the mining community.[249] As the Sergeant had replaced the second Constable, this may have led to the re-instatement of the latter post by September 1871, so there were then as many officers at Rosedale as at Pickering. It's also possible that sometime, as the workload steadily increased, that the Sergeant was provided with a horse.[250]

The type and frequency of the incidents which typically occurred in Rosedale illustrate how the workload in the area was generated.

As early as April 1861 there was a report of what appears to have been 'prize' fighting, or at least some sort of contest probably connected with gambling. Similarly, the following month there was horse racing, an activity notorious for the sometimes accompanying 'trouble'.[251] In June 1862 serious fighting between large groups of English and Irish labourers was reported – many had received severe injuries.[252]

Although such crimes occurred regularly anyway, in November that year three cases of robbery or burglary were reported in a single week.[253] In another week, in October 1867, burglary was attempted at one Rosedale residence and succeeded at another.[254] In February 1869 the landlord of a Rosedale beer house was knocked unconscious during a violent assault by a group of passing drunks he refused to serve after permitted hours.[255] In November of that year the Pickering magistrates took several hours to hear cases of assault, in what seems to have been a mass brawl at a Rosedale inn.[256]

In August 1870 several men were found guilty of fighting on the highway.[257] As they'd stripped (to the waist) to fight and were being watched by a large crowd this may have been another case of 'prize' fighting. The Constable on duty, in Rosedale on a Saturday night in July 1871, was severely assaulted, after trying to break up a fight between two miners.[258] In one week in February 1873 most of the fifteen cases of drunkenness at Pickering Petty Sessions originated from Rosedale.[259]

Formally, part of Rosedale lay within the Ryedale district, but it isn't surprising, in the light of the type of incidents related that, when the latter was re-allocated to the Malton Division, Pickering Lythe retained responsibility for the area. Pickering was closer, in the event that re-enforcements were needed, and Supt. Jonas had plenty of experience of what was involved in policing Rosedale.

However, reflecting the increasing problem that the area was becoming, and the impact of 'losing' the Inspector at Kirkbymoorside, an Inspector's post was added to the Establishment for Rosedale from March 1873.

The *Illustrated Police News* reported, in February 1874, that a major brawl had taken place in Rosedale after a miner had been arrested.[260]

There was more interest however in another miner who'd eventually been apprehended in Dalton in Furness (between Ulverston and Barrow in what was then north-west Lancashire), whose fine and costs at Pickering amounted to £20, which was being met, half each, by the Dalton and Rosedale miners, to avoid the alternative four months' hard labour.[261]

In June that year a miner, who'd returned to work after an accident, was assaulted by three men who reportedly were involved in an industrial dispute elsewhere in the dale.[262] As the three concluded the attack by throwing the victim over a wall and pushing the coping stones on to him, he was fortunate to be alive. A warrant was issued for the arrest of the assailants, who were 'known', and after one was captured, the Inspector at Rosedale telegraphed Supt. Jonas for assistance to search the mines, as one of the others was suspected to be hiding below ground.[263] The first man arrested was fined £3 and around a month later the other two were apprehended and fined the same – all three denied that the assault was related to the industrial dispute. The magistrates commented that the sentences would have been far more severe if they'd thought that intimidation had been involved, but it didn't stop an almost identical case only two years later, when two miners tried to stop another working overtime.[264] As they attempted to drag him out of the mine, they'd entered without permission, his colleagues apprehended them. The mining company presumably didn't want to further inflame what was obviously a fraught situation, so didn't press charges of intimidation, and the trespassers were only fined £1 each plus costs.

In August 1874 three miners assaulted the Inspector and a Constable after being told to go home quietly.[265] Having heard that the attack involved large stones, taken from a wall, the magistrates described the assault as one of the worst from the area that had come before them, and fined each defendant £6, plus costs, although they were unable to pay so took the alternative two months' imprisonment.

Even after production had peaked and the workforce had begun to decline, at a single Petty Sessions in January 1875, two miners were fined with costs, for obstructing the highway by fighting, another was charged with assaulting the landlord of a Rosedale inn and a fourth with refusing to leave the same establishment.[266]

The *York Herald* commented, in June 1876, that the usually expected number of Rosedale miners had appeared at the Petty Sessions and had been dealt with in the usually expected way. The magistrates were told that closing public houses would not solve the problem, as the miners simply went to what were essentially 'off' licenses, where they were able to buy kegs of beer and/or bottles of spirits at any time of the day.

As well as assaults, burglary, drunkenness, fighting, gambling and highway robbery, other vices obviously proliferated with an itinerant prostitute being given seven days' hard labour for plying her trade in August 1871.[267]

While Rosedale was a continuing issue there were of course, incidents elsewhere in the Division.

In December 1861 a property in Wrelton was broken into, between £2 and £3 in coins stolen from the till (cash register), and the premises ransacked.[268]

On examining the scene, the police discovered that the culprit had left foot prints and the marks of a false leg, no doubt immediately leading to a short list of local suspects. Presumably after asking about the recent spending habits of those individuals he knew to be missing a leg, the following day Supt. Jonas apprehended a man, who, on the afternoon of the break-in, had bought a clarinet in Wrelton for 8s (40p). The suspect had also bought ale at a local inn before travelling to Pickering, where he'd visited the Railway Tavern in Park Street before moving to the Spotted Cow on the Whitby Road. He'd also paid a small amount to a local book seller. After admitting that he'd stolen 13s 6d (67½p), the man was committed to the next Quarter Sessions, where a theft in Pickering the previous November was also taken into account and he was sentenced to eighteen months' hard labour.[269]

In April 1862 Supt. Jonas was involved in the long distance pursuit of an offender, after a farmer from Butterwick, around 9 miles south-west of Pickering, was robbed by two men, who'd also attempted to throw him into a river.[270] As the names of the men were 'known', John would have had descriptions of them, but would have needed to make enquiries at every point where they may have varied their escape route, as he followed them from one place to the next.[271]

There are contemporary accounts of police officers travelling long distances on foot, and John may have done likewise in this case. By walking he'd more easily have the opportunity to engage anyone he encountered, as well as people in shops and inns, in 'small' talk. He might have continued such conversations for some time, occasionally introducing 'innocent' questions to discover more of his quarry.

This approach would probably have been made easier, as would listening to conversations, particularly those in 'foreign' accents, if he wasn't wearing uniform.[272] Hopefully he'd eventually locate his suspect, as he did in this case in a Sheffield pub, a fortnight after the offence.[273] John took the man to Pickering where he was committed for trial at York Assizes. In July he was sentenced to twelve months' imprisonment. Meanwhile, Supt. Jonas followed the other suspect to Liverpool, but he'd sailed for America shortly before John arrived.[274]

Poaching was a major issue throughout the country and the North Riding was no exception. In early September 1863 there was a major confrontation between three poachers and two game keepers on the estate of Lord Feversham, near Helmsley. This led to both game keepers being badly injured, one near fatally, and Feversham offering a £25 reward for the capture of a William Harper and a Thomas Jackson. It was reported that the poachers had escaped to Bridlington, around 35 miles south-east of Pickering, before travelling to Norton, near Malton, where Harper had separated from his accomplices. He then presumably walked around six miles to his sister's in Great Barugh, which was where, acting on information received, Supt. Jonas found him in bed and arrested him. After initially being held at Pickering, he was taken to Helmsley, where he appeared at the Petty Sessions, charged with intent to murder one of the gamekeepers.[275]

Suggesting that a description, if not a drawing of the wanted man had been circulated locally, in November, with the help of the Superintendent of the Bulmer Division, based at Clifton near York, Jackson was arrested in Market Weighton (in the East Riding) where he was working on the extension of the York – Beverley railway line.

He was taken to Pickering by the Constable from Helmsley, who'd made the arrest, and handed over to Supt. Jonas before appearing with Harper the following month at the winter Assizes in York.[276]

The defence argued that the poachers hadn't planned to attack the gamekeepers, and had only been trying to defend themselves, as the latter were armed and had a dog. Harper claimed to have only retaliated after the lesser injured keeper had assaulted him, but was imprisoned for eighteen months for unlawful wounding.

Jackson was found guilty of wounding with intent to do grievous bodily harm. As he'd been imprisoned for six months previously for night poaching and wounding, and on other occasions for assaults and offences against the game (poaching) laws, he was sentenced to six years' penal servitude.[277]

In February 1864 there was an accident on the Whitby & Pickering railway line, when the cable used to lower trains down the approximate 1,500 yard (1,370 m) incline from Goathland to Beckhole snapped, while in use.[278]

Two people were killed and ten seriously injured, but Supt. Jonas probably had little involvement as, although the incident happened inside the Pickering Division, close to the blast furnaces at Beckhole, a Whitby Division officer was the first attendee and the bodies were taken to Whitby.

However, the accident would have impacted on railway operations, and the link through the Moors to Whitby may have been interrupted, until May 1865 when a 4½ mile 'deviation' line was opened, together with a new station at Goathland (Mill).[279]

Two of John's slightly more unusual cases were reported in June 1864.

Following the theft of £30 cash and £420 worth of bonds from the home of the schoolmaster in Newton, around 5 miles north of Pickering, Supt. Jonas examined the scene but, apart from a broken window, found no sign of entry.

Possibly because the 'usual' indicators were absent, he concluded that the theft involved someone who lived in the house and learning that the schoolmaster's wife had moved out, traced her to Thornton (Dale). After discovering that she had substantial funds, Supt. Jonas accused her of theft, which after an initial denial, she admitted.[280]

Around the same time, £105 cash was stolen from the desk of a farmer in Great Habton, around 6 miles south of Pickering. The farmer and his family were at their local chapel when a female servant arrived to tell them that thieves were in their house. The servant later told Supt. Jonas that she'd heard a noise, which had led her to discover the farmer's desk being robbed by three men, one of whom had thrown a 'chisel' at her, as she escaped.[281]

Neighbours were questioned but none had seen any men or heard any noise. Supt. Jonas examined the desk and discovered that it had been marked to make it appear that an entry had been forced, but that the marks were not like those usually made when a 'chisel' was used in such a way. He concluded that the lock hadn't been forced, but undone using the key usually kept in an under drawer. After questioning the servant again, and receiving inconsistent responses, Supt. Jonas began to suspect that she was the thief, so he arrested her and took her into custody at Pickering.

The following day one of the farmer's labourers found all of the money under the roof tiles of a farm outbuilding, adding weight to the view that the 17 year old servant's tale of the three men was false. At the Midsummer Quarter Sessions, at the end of June, she was sentenced to twelve months' imprisonment.[282]

In August 1864 Supt. Jonas was called to investigate the robbery of clothing from a shop in Rosedale Abbey. After the suspected thieves were described to him, John realised that he'd seen men who matched the descriptions, a short time before.

Presumably, as a result of asking people in the vicinity who might also have seen the suspects, he set out after them in the direction of Whitby. As it was summer at least he probably didn't have to battle the elements but the journey itself would have been challenging. Moving along pathways, and maybe odd stretches of unmade road, he'd have to cross open moorland, broken by occasional streams and areas of soft ground, before descending into the relatively benign Esk valley. Even following the most direct route John probably covered around 20 miles before reaching Whitby.

After no doubt making enquiries and seeking descriptions at pawnbrokers and second hand shops; also at inns and lodging houses, he apprehended one of the suspects and, after finding some of the stolen clothing on him, took the man to Pickering.[283] He received six months' imprisonment at the next Quarter Sessions.[284]

During May 1865 Supt. Jonas was called to Oswaldkirk where the body of a baby had been found in the well of the local rector.[285]

John apparently questioned all of the employees in the house, leading him to apprehend one of the females, after the cook claimed that six months earlier the latter had been pregnant. The cook and the kitchen maid had also mentioned that the suspect had been ill three weeks previously.

Supt. Jonas took the woman to Helmsley, where she confessed that she was the mother of the baby, and had delivered it in the water closet. After a hearing at the Petty Sessions in Helmsley, during which all of the relevant evidence already given at an Inquest was repeated, and the assistant Coroner described the baby as having been still born, the woman was committed for trial at the next Assizes in York.[286]

In August, on the grounds that the child hadn't been alive at birth, and that she'd been incarcerated since early May, the woman was sentenced to two months' imprisonment - less than she might have been expected to receive.[287]

A case in January 1866, at Pickering, involved three boys who'd been throwing stones which had led to windows being broken. Each boy was ordered to receive six strokes across the bare back with a birch rod.[288] This would have been inflicted by the police, most likely in the police station, or station yard, and almost certainly in the presence of Supt. Jonas.[289]

Of course, while he had incidents such as these to contend with, John would also have had to continue with his ongoing responsibilities, such as the various non police inspections and the administrative tasks, including completion of several accounts and the numerous returns, required by the Chief Constable.

While many of these tasks were probably undertaken when time allowed during his working 'day', that wouldn't always have been possible with others, such as attending Petty Sessions, Quarter Sessions or occasionally Assizes.

Petty Sessions may not have involved much more than a few hours on a Monday in Pickering, but occasionally the Superintendent had to attend Helmsley or Scarborough, which may have involved the best part of a day, with the travelling involved. Attending the other courts, in Northallerton or York, would have involved using the train, and sometimes staying overnight if an early attendance was required, or a late finish anticipated.

John would also have had to travel, and no doubt probably stay overnight, when he was required to attend events/incidents some distance away from Pickering. However, potentially the greatest travelling demands would have been those relating to meeting his Constables, (Sergeants) and Inspectors, and visiting his townships, particularly as this was a continuing requirement. The Ayton Inspector managed to visit Staintondale within a long day, but for John visiting locations east of Ayton and west of Kirkbymoorside may have required overnight stays. This may explain why, at least during the period of the *Journal*, he didn't seem to have visited these areas unless there was a specific event/incident.

Whenever he did travel it's probable that, when he could, he'd have used the train, and with the availability of horse boxes, then part of many rural rail services, may on some occasions also have taken his horse. It isn't difficult to envisage him travelling on the train to Rillington and from there to York (usually for onward connections), or to Scarborough and then riding to his final destination.

As he patrolled Pickering, and/or travelled around his district, Supt. Jonas was also involved in minor cases.

In June 1868 he charged a farm labourer from Welburn, some 1½ miles south-west of Kirkbymoorside, with being drunk and incapable.[290] The Superintendent had found the labourer collapsed in front of his horses at Aislaby, around 2½ miles west of Pickering, presumably on his way home after being to the latter, where he'd got drunk. Costs of 11s (55p) were awarded.[291]

In November the same year a farmer on his way home from the Pickering 'hirings' was approached by a woman who threw her arms around him, allowing her male accomplice to take between £11 and £12 from his pockets. The farmer didn't report the robbery until the next day, but Supt. Jonas was able to trace the couple to Lockton, around 6 miles north of Pickering, where they'd apparently arrived some three hours after the incident and had begun spending extravagantly at the local inn.

They were found sleeping in nearby woodlands, in the early hours of the next morning, and taken to Pickering where, despite almost all of the stolen money being recovered, the female was sentenced to two months' and the male to three (both hard labour).[292]

The following month, Thornton (Dale) surgeon Donald Robertson, was called to the Marishes home of John Dodsworth and his family, around 4 miles south of Pickering. Several people, particularly John's wife Elizabeth, had suffered violent sickness combined, in some cases, with a burning sensation in their stomachs. The doctor diagnosed poisoning, and discovered that the food or liquid consumed by all of those affected was coffee.

As it was easier to introduce an undetectable 'foreign' element into the sugar, than into the coffee, Robertson obviously suspected the former. As a result he analysed a sample of the sugar and discovered that *tartar emetic* and *nitrate of potash* (kept for treating horses) had been mixed into it. These elements would have produced the symptoms which most of the family had suffered, and as the 12 year old servant had refused to have sugar in her coffee, Mr. Robertson took her to Supt. Jonas at the police station in Pickering.

If Supt. Jonas didn't already know the girl he knew of her as he'd recently investigated a case that she'd been involved in, which was going to court the following month.

There an 11 year old girl, her 13 year old brother and a 12 year old girl were accused of stealing from a Pickering wine merchant. In evidence for the prosecution, the 11 year old described how she'd stayed outside the shop as a look out, while the other girl went inside and distracted the counter staff. This allowed the 12 year old and the boy to pick up what they could and leave the shop. Supt. Jonas had established that using this technique, in which they'd apparently been schooled by the servant now accused of poisoning, they'd managed to carry out substantial thefts from almost every shop in the town. The boy and the 12 year old girl were gaoled for a month each while the 11 year old was discharged as she'd given evidence.[293]

Supt. Jonas now asked the young servant if she'd added poison to the sugar. She confirmed that she knew that it was poison, because Mr Dodsworth had told her, and that she had mixed it with the sugar, but added that she'd only done it in retaliation against the farm boys, who'd been chastising her.

After appearing at Pickering Petty Sessions in early January, the girl was committed for trial at the next Quarter Sessions, on a charge of maliciously administering poison to inflict bodily harm.[294]

After hearing all of the evidence, it was explained to the Quarter Sessions jury that they had to decide the degree of guilt of the accused. She might have administered the poison with the intent of doing grievous bodily harm to the family, knowing the effect that it was likely to have, or to have done nothing more than to mix the poison with the sugar, to annoy the farm boys. The jury found the girl guilty of the latter - a misdemeanor.[295] After the verdict the (Quarter Sessions) magistrates stated that they couldn't see that sending such a young girl to prison would produce any beneficial effect. Instead they admonished her, pointing out the atrocious nature of the offence, and sentenced her to a days' imprisonment. Presumably on the grounds that she'd been incarcerated for some time before the trial, the sentence must have been considered as served and the magistrates instructed Supt. Jonas to take the girl home to her mother.[296]

In late 1869 a slightly unusual case was covered by the *Illustrated Police News*. The 16 year old driver of tramway horses in the East Rosedale mines had struck an overseer, whose skull was fractured, and who later died from tetanus. The Inquest jury returned a verdict of Wilful Murder against the boy and the Coroner committed him for trial at the next Assizes. However, the committal magistrates decided that the 16 year old was only guilty of manslaughter, and when the case was heard at the Assizes the judge expressed the view that they were probably correct and directed that the charge should be changed.

The boy subsequently pleaded guilty to manslaughter and was sentenced to six months' imprisonment.[297]

Based on information received, in August 1870 Supt. Jonas went to Great Barugh, around 6 miles south of Pickering, where he questioned a woman about a baby. She told him that she'd given birth, but that the baby didn't move or cry, and that she'd wrapped it in a petticoat and buried it in the garden. Supt. Jonas located the grave and found the body around 12 inches (300 mm) below the surface. He took the woman into custody and conveyed her and the body of the female baby to Pickering where, on behalf of the Coroner, the latter was examined by a local doctor. He reported that there was no mark on the body and that he believed that the baby had reached maturity, and might have survived if the woman had been properly attended during the birth. A magistrate then committed the woman to the next York Assizes on a charge of concealment of birth.[298] At the Gaol Delivery in December the 35 year old was sentenced to three months' imprisonment.[299]

In early January 1871 a man staying at a lodging house in Pickering was robbed of a coat, scarves and boots and of 4s 6d (22½p) cash. Supt. Jonas traced a man who'd stayed at the house on the same night, but who'd left before daybreak heading for Lofthouse, where he was arrested, the Superintendent having found the boots 'in pledge' in Whitby (21 days' hard labour).[300]

In June that year the *York Herald* reported that the Chief Constable had examined the new clothing (uniform) being worn by the officers in Pickering Lythe. Replacement items were distributed annually in conformance with the *Rules*, which stipulated the issue required on a two year alternating cycle.[301]

However in this case, the inspection by the Chief Constable, which the *Journal* suggests wasn't unusual, may have been prompted by the distribution of some new, rather than replacement, uniform.[302]

Although the circumstances might have been unusual, in October 1871 John and Eleanor may have attended the wedding of John (George) in Holborn (in the City of London).[303]

In May 1872, and possibly not unconnected with the Licensing Act of that year, Supt. Jonas charged the landlords of the Black Bull, Kings Arms and Buck Inn at Thornton (Dale), with sales during prohibited hours (on a Sunday).[304] He also charged the landlord of the Golden Lion at Great Barugh with permitting drunkenness and supplying alcohol to a drunk.[305]

# CROPTON

One Thursday in May 1872, John Wood, a farmer from Cropton Lane, between Wrelton and Cropton, and his brother William, asked Supt. Jonas to contact the police in Liverpool, in regard to their brother Joseph, another farmer.

John, who lived around 300 yards (270m) from Joseph, hadn't seen the latter since the previous Friday.[306] However, on the Saturday he'd been told by Robert Charter, a cousin from Lastingham, around 2 miles north-west of Cropton, who'd been living at Joseph's farm since the previous Monday, that Joseph and his eldest son, also Joseph, had gone away for a few days.[307]

It had seemed strange to John Wood that his brother hadn't told him, or it seemed anyone else other than Charter, that he was going away, then that Thursday the latter had shown him a letter from Joseph. Supposedly written in Liverpool and dated (Monday) 20 May, the letter asked Charter to settle Joseph's affairs, as he was going overseas. However, John Wood didn't believe that the handwriting was Joseph's so he'd gone to see his brother William, a grocer and draper in Pickering. They'd telegraphed a Liverpool shipping agent, to ask if Joseph's name was on any passenger list, before approaching Supt. Jonas.

The next day, Friday 24 May, the Superintendent, together with William Wood, went to John Wood's to tell him that no signs of Joseph, and no clue, could be found.

Following that, as Joseph Wood had a reputation for being 'eccentric', and as William and John couldn't swear that the 'Liverpool' letter wasn't in their brother's handwriting (it contained apologies for being written in haste and with a 'poor' pen), Supt. Jonas presumably considered that he couldn't do anything further.[308]

After his brother in law suggested that he should speak to Charter again, on Saturday 3 August John Wood, accompanied by Supt. Jonas, went to Joseph Wood's farm, which Charter had continued to run.

Supt. Jonas asked to see the 'Liverpool' letter and then enquired if there were any cellars, wells or such places. He searched the bedrooms and the cellar but found nothing, although as he continued to lack any evidence of a crime his search was probably not as exhaustive as it could have been.[309]

According to John Wood, Supt. Jonas then questioned Charter intensively. However, the responses and lack of evidence were presumably such that the Superintendent again took no further action, and/or decided to await developments.

During that summer, John Jonas's attention was probably at least partly distracted by the impending marriage of his youngest daughter, Julia, to Watson Mortimer, a local man and coincidentally a draper's assistant in William Wood's shop.[310]

In mid September, Robert Charter called at William Wood's on Market Place, with an offer to relinquish Joseph's farm, and a few days later it was agreed that the property would be handed over to John Wood.

On Saturday 2 November, a pair of shoes fell from some straw which John Wood, and one of his labourers, were throwing from a barn on Joseph Wood's farm. John didn't know where the shoes were from but their discovery obviously aroused his suspicions as the following day he, and his wife, again searched Joseph's house. In a hole under the stairs, which hadn't been searched previously, a pair of 'Sunday' boots, which they thought might be Joseph's, were found.

John Wood checked with the shoe maker in Appleton le Moor(s), but the latter couldn't recall having made any boots for Joseph for some time. Meanwhile, William Wood checked with a retailer of factory made boots in Pickering but the latter didn't recollect Joseph making any recent purchase, so John Wood concluded that the shoes and boots which he'd found couldn't have been made redundant by a new pair.

On the Monday, John Wood and his son 'dragged' the pond in the pasture behind Joseph Wood's farm buildings, and found parts of a coat and of a white linen shirt and some woollen corded trousers. As a result they went to Pickering and informed Supt. Jonas who asked them to look after the items and to arrange a pump to drain the pond.

The following day, as the pond was being emptied, Supt. Jonas, who'd been watching, noticed a left hand, followed by a pair of trousers in the pocket of which was 4s (20p). Soon after those discoveries, the front and back of a black cloth waistcoat and small portion of a coat were found. Following this, Supt. Jonas must have reported the findings to the Chief Constable because the next day the latter telegraphed Inspector Nicholson at Thirsk, instructing him to assist Supt. Jonas.

On Wednesday 6 November, presumably during a much more thorough search of Joseph Wood's house than he'd made in August, Supt. Jonas found a boy's jacket and waistcoat under the bottom step of the stairs leading to the loft. He then found a pair of boy's boots hidden under the boiler in the farm's boiler house.

The following day, Supt. Jonas directed a search of the rest of the premises, including the orchard where there was a large stack of brushwood underneath which the Superintendent noticed that the earth had recently been disturbed. He instructed officers to excavate the area. Between 12 and 15 inches (300 – 380 mm) below the surface a right hand and two feet were found, in a position which suggested that they'd previously been attached to a body, which had been laid on its back, in what was essentially a shallow grave. Supt. Jonas inferred from this that the limbs had become detached when the body that they belonged to had been moved. He also matched the scraps of clothing still on the feet with what had been recovered from the pond earlier in the week.

Later that day, Jonas and Nicholson (who'd arrived on the night of Wednesday 6 November) went to Robert Charter's house in Lastingham. As Supt. Jonas would have been aware that victims generally knew their assailants, and that the last person to see a victim was, in most cases, usually their killer, Charter was the most likely suspect.[311] Presumably after further questioning, Charter was charged with murdering Joseph Wood on (Friday) 17 May. The house was searched and Supt. Jonas discovered an envelope and a sheet of paper which matched that used for the 'Liverpool' letter, obviously providing further evidence against Charter.

The same day Supt. Jonas questioned one of Charter's sons in law, William Hardwick, a farmer from Lastingham. He was questioned again several times during the following week, including on Sunday 10 November when he provided a false alibi regarding his whereabouts on the nights of 21 and 22 May.

Further searches were made during the following days, although Supt. Jonas and his local team were otherwise engaged on Monday 11 November, as that was the day of the Pickering Martinmas 'hirings'.[312]

The next day Supt. Jonas and Insp. Nicholson went to the fields farmed by Robert Charter, around ½ mile from Lastingham, in search of a site where they'd been informed that Charter and Hardwick had been seen spreading earth. The two locations that they initially examined presumably yielded nothing, but Supt. Jonas noticed some recently disturbed ground, at the lower end of the gently downward sloping field, on the opposite side of the road (from Cropton). After finding a spade and a fork close by, the two officers began excavating the earth which filled what had been the meander of a stream. Around 36 inches (920 mm) below the surface they discovered a sack, which they took to Pickering police station after finding that it contained part of a body. By this time Robert Charter was in a cell at the police station so he probably soon heard about the discovery of the body or may even have seen it being washed and examined in the police station yard.[313]

After being given the 'usual caution' ("that what he said might be brought against him") on Wednesday (13 November) Charter gave a statement to Supt. Jonas and Insp. Nicholson.

He claimed that he'd found Joseph Wood's body and concealed it, first in the barn, and then under the brushwood in the orchard, as he was concerned that he might be blamed for murdering Joseph. To cover up the disappearances he'd written the bogus letter and given it to a man, from Rosedale, who'd been passing on his way to Liverpool.[314] The following day, in the absence of Supt. Jonas, Charter made another statement, to Acting Sergeant Silversides, in which he described how he'd hit Joseph Wood with an (iron) bar and how he'd been provoked to this attack. He claimed not to have killed Joseph deliberately and that he'd never seen the boy.

The same day Supt. Jonas apprehended William Hardwick who denied any part in the murder but admitted taking the bogus letter to Liverpool, which resulted in him being charged as an accessory after the fact.

As no remains of the boy had been found, the Inquest, on Saturday 16 November, was solely into the death of Joseph Wood.[315] Lasting from 10 a.m. until after 6 p.m., evidence was heard which confirmed that the body was Joseph Wood's and established the probable cause of his death. After all of the witnesses had appeared, Charter was given an opportunity to explain his position to the jury but didn't add anything.[316] In his summary, the Coroner told the jury that Joseph Wood had been violently murdered and that it was for them to decide who was responsible for this. He also pointed out that the boy's body hadn't been found and told them that they were not being asked to consider, what he thought must also have been, another violent death. Following a fifteen minute adjournment, the jury's unanimous verdict was Wilful Murder, after which the Coroner made out a warrant of commitment for trial at the next York Assizes.[317]

On the same day as the Inquest, police and volunteers, under the direction of Supt. Jonas, continued their search for the boy, moving from Charter's fields at Lastingham to Joseph Wood's at Cropton Lane.

Manure had been heaped in one of the fields and on spreading this they found bones which were identified as coming from a right thigh, a left leg and a shoulder. The following day, Supt. Jonas, now knowing where and what to look for, found a small rib in manure on another field.[318]

If the case wasn't already well known it now became infamous. The new finds, in particular, generated a great deal of excitement throughout the country as the story featured in all of the national daily newspapers.[319]

The press, and no doubt local gossip, speculated as to how the bones had got into the manure. Many believed that the boy's body had been (boiled and) fed to the eight pigs kept on Joseph Wood's farm, particularly as, according to local sources, these were so neglected that their condition had caused neighbours' concerns.

Before Charter and Hardwick went to the Assizes they had to face examination by the local magistrates, which began on Monday 25 November. The charge against Charter was of the murder of Joseph Wood and that against Hardwick was of harbouring Charter, knowing that he had committed murder.

Robert Dale, barrister, prosecuted on behalf of the Chief Constable, who was present in the court, but there was no defence, despite Supt. Jonas having pointed this out to Charter and giving him an opportunity to make appropriate arrangements.

John Wood, Thomas Stead, John Dobson, Charlotte Ann Thompson and William Wood gave identification evidence and a narrative of events, as at the Inquest, to five magistrates. Other witnesses, such as David Morrill, corroborated Thomas Stead's evidence. John Braithwaite and John and Jane Garbutt gave evidence regarding Hardwick being in Malton on Tuesday 21 and Thursday 23 May, but missing from there, presumed to be elsewhere, on Wednesday 22 May.

Evidence from Thomas Overington and Ursula and John Trowsdale concerned sightings of Charter (and Hardwick) in late October, or early November, in or near the field where Joseph Wood's body had been found. Charles Bosomworth, Thomas Berriman and Robert Wood gave evidence regarding the discovery of the bones in the manure. Thomas Kirby described how Hardwick had asked him for an alibi for around the time of Kirkbymoorside 'fair' – 22 May and Hannah Hutchison recalled a visit by Charter to the Hardwick household in the early hours of one morning in May. Substantial evidence was given by Supt. Jonas (and later corroborated by Insp. Nicholson).

Dr. Walker described the remains of Joseph Wood, the injuries he'd noted and how they might have been made, evidence supported by a Pickering surgeon, Mr. Scholefield, who'd examined the body with him.

The doctor also described the four bones found in the manure on Joseph Wood's farm and suggested that they were probably from a child of between 8 and 10 years. However, although Joseph was, or had been, 8 years old, Walker couldn't go beyond that in terms of identification.

In his opinion the bones had been gnawed by dogs or pigs.

Charter and Hardwick were asked if they had any response to the charges and the former admitted striking Joseph Wood once, but denied that it was wilful, with an intention to kill, adding that Hardwick had nothing to do with the murder.

Following two 'full' days of testimony, both men were committed for trial at the following Spring Assizes.

On Wednesday 27 November the court 'sat' again to hear the same charges which had been levelled in respect of Joseph Wood, put in relation to his son Joseph Thompson.

During this trial, Thomas Stead, a butcher who'd been working on Joseph Wood's farm, admitted, under cross examination from Charter, that he'd taken some 'beef' from the cellar and thrown it to the pigs, because it smelt. However, he was unable to say when that had happened, other than it was during the summer. After a recall, Stead related that about three weeks after Joseph Wood had gone missing, he'd seen several pigs pulling at something like a piece of flesh at the top of the manure heap. This was after the 'beef' which smelt had been thrown to the pigs, but it hadn't occurred to him that it could be the same piece of meat.

After a second day, the Chairman of the magistrates stated that the 'bench' unanimously committed Charter and Hardwick for trial on the respective charges.

On Friday 29 November, in another major police operation, designed to evade the large, often hostile, crowds which had accompanied every movement of Charter and Hardwick, they were taken to Pickering railway station. From there they travelled, via Malton, to York and the Castle prison.[320]

Court attendances and crowd management responsibilities might have been over but the search for the boy's body continued and despite inclement weather, including snow, occupied most of December. Supt. Jonas directed the excavation of every part of the orchard at Cropton Lane, although other sites on the farm and at Lastingham were also examined.

With the most dramatic episode of the Cropton Murders case, as it became known, behind them, reverting to their normal activities as 1873 began must, at the least, have seemed anti-climactic for Supt. Jonas and his colleagues in Pickering Lythe.

However, if nothing else occupied them, the Rosedale 'issue' continued, with the prosecution of a licensee for permitting drunkenness, and a watch theft, subsequent arrest and hearing reported by the *York Herald* in February.[321] Supt. Jonas would also no doubt have had some involvement in the transfer of the Ryedale district to the Malton Division in the same month.

In March, Supt. Jonas and some of his colleagues had to attend the Spring Assizes in York, for the trial of Charter and Hardwick.[322]

On Saturday 22 March the Grand Jury dismissed the charges against them in relation to the boy, Joseph Thompson, through lack of evidence, other than the few bones found (which didn't amount to identification).[323] Essentially, without an identifiable body it was not possible at this time to prove that any crime had been committed. When the Assizes trial started, on Tuesday 25 March, the charges against Charter and Hardwick were therefore only those relating to Joseph Wood.

In the presence of a Lord Chief Justice and a comprehensive, professional, legal defence for the accused, the trial lasted two days.

As with the Inquest, and magistrates' hearings, the case was widely and comprehensively reported, in some instances almost verbatim.

The range of witnesses was largely as before but there was much more probing in regard to Joseph Wood's mental condition and to Charter's statements and an amendment he'd asked to be made to the first of these. Conflicts regarding the identification of Charter and Hardwick, near where Joseph Wood's body had been found, were also challenged. This was due to there being less certainty in the statements now being provided, and any other such uncertainties were also rigorously examined. The medical evidence from Doctors Walker and Scholefield, in particular that relating to the number of blows to the skull, and whether these were pre or post death, was also tested in detail.

On the afternoon of Wednesday 26 March counsel began summing up. Charter's defence warned the jury not to convict on anything related to the disappearance of the boy as the Grand Jury had ruled any evidence regarding that (and the discovery of clothes and bones) as irrelevant.

Counsel also pointed to a lack of motive and to the efforts Charter had put into running the farm, yet voluntarily handing it back to the Wood family. He claimed that the manner and circumstances of the death did not mean anything underhand or premeditated, and suggested that it was a case of manslaughter rather than murder.

Hardwick's defence claimed that he was simply guilty of telling a lie and that it hadn't occurred to him that there was anything wrong in going to Liverpool and posting the bogus letter. His presence in the field with Charter was not unusual, given that he regularly worked for him. He had acted foolishly but in ignorance of any crime.

Beginning his summary of the case, the judge advised the jury that they must have no doubts before giving a verdict of guilty, but that they could choose an alternative of manslaughter.[324] This would be appropriate if they believed Charter's second statement, regarding how Joseph Wood had been abusing him, including with a gun, and how he'd retaliated by striking Wood. The judge explained the difference between murder and manslaughter in detail and, after reviewing the defence arguments at length, told the jury that these should be carefully considered.

The judge then read all of the evidence to the jury, mentioning that however Charter's first statement might have been altered (this had been a major point of contention during the trial), or not, didn't change the substantive meaning of the statement, or what should be inferred from it. In regard to Hardwick, the judge explained that there was no positive evidence to show that he was aware of the murder, or that he had assisted in hiding the body.

The jury retired at 7:45 p.m. and returned 35 minutes later.

Charter was found guilty of manslaughter. However, as there couldn't be any justification for the level of force used to strike the deceased, and because his attempts at concealing the crime seriously aggravated the original offence, he was sentenced to twenty years' penal servitude. Hardwick was found not guilty.[325]

Subsequently there was some disquiet over the verdict on Charter and over the lack of prosecution for the presumed death of the boy.

The day following the end of the trial, the *Leeds Mercury* for example, pointed out that, based on the evidence of Charter, he was guilty of either justifiable homicide, or murder, but not manslaughter. The same day the *Bradford Observer* was critical over the failure to address the probability that Joseph Thompson had also suffered a violent death.

As far as is known, nothing further occurred in regard to the missing boy, although a careful watch was kept for possible remains when the site of Charter's home in Lastingham was re-developed for a new school in 1885.[326]

# RETURN TO NORMAL?

In September 1873, John (George) re-joined the North Riding Constabulary, serving in the Northallerton, and later the Langbaurgh West Divisions, for the next 25 years.[327]

During 1874, having connected Helmsley and Kirkbymoorside to the rail network, the new line from Gilling continued to progress towards Pickering.[328] Like those who'd constructed the lines into Rosedale the previous decade, the itinerant 'navvy' workforce constructing the railway, no doubt presented a variety of problems to the police and local communities. The section to Pickering was finally opened in April 1875, probably adding to the frustrations felt by the town's population over the closing of roads by level crossing gates, and the noise (and smoke) produced by the regular shunting of carriages and wagons.[329]

The completed line would also have had implications for the police as it was likely to bring more visitors particularly as, due to anticipated new customers, it had been agreed with Helmsley and Kirkbymoorside that weekly agricultural produce, and fortnightly livestock, markets would be re-established at the three towns.

Despite this increased potential for new incidents, in April 1876, Supt. Jonas presented a clear charge sheet at Pickering Petty Sessions, there being no cases anywhere in his district for the first time in fourteen years.[330]

At the beginning of October 1876, Eleanor Jonas died, while at the home of her youngest daughter, in Loftus.[331]

Julia had moved to the town after her marriage and it's not unreasonable to believe that Eleanor might have been a regular visitor, particularly after a granddaughter was born in 1873.[332] On the other hand, she may have gone there with an ailment, to be nursed by her daughter.[333]

Whatever the reasons for her presence, it seems that Eleanor may have been at Julia's for some time as the certifying doctor was able to state how long each of her afflictions had existed, and the apparent lack of an Inquest suggests that their outcome wasn't unexpected.[334]

While it seems probable that Eleanor's death was 'natural', it must have been a major shock as her life expectancy was likely to have been significantly greater than the 60 years she'd probably recently celebrated.[335]

Unsurprisingly, the effect on John of his wife's death must have been devastating - in early November he was reduced to Superintendent 2nd class for neglect of duty.[336] A fortnight later he was reduced to Inspector for the same reason, although it seems that he was continuing in his usual role, as around the same time it was reported that he'd been sworn in at Pickering Petty Sessions.[337]

'De-ranking' to Inspector may have been a consequence of a situation, but it might equally have been in anticipation, as it meant that John could no longer hold his position in Pickering, and at the beginning of December the *Malton Messenger* reported that he was being 'removed' to Yarm.

This probably wasn't unduly severe as the only other options available to the Chief Constable, in the light of John apparently being unable to continue at Pickering (or as a Superintendent), were probably dismissal or retirement.

Capt. Hill may have resisted the former, in the light of John's service, and because it would have led to what would probably have been a key reason for John wishing to avoid retirement – having his former working hours suddenly unoccupied, at the very time he'd least want to be in that position.

After he'd served there in 1860, the continuing growth of South Stockton had led to the town being provided with a lock up.[338] However by the end of 1865, with only two cells, that was reported as being too small and causing overcrowding at Yarm so, after various delays, South Stockton had been provided with a new police station.[339]

Another reason for this would have been the growth of the force in the town since John had been the incumbent Sergeant. This had been in response to the growth of population, leading to the county providing additional officers, and the establishment of several major industrial enterprises which funded Constables, although numbers had fluctuated, presumably as the latter's requirements changed. By the time John arrived in Yarm the total number of Constables supporting the Sergeant in South Stockton may have been in excess of twelve or thirteen.

As part of their deliberations about a new station, the Police Committee had proposed moving the Petty Sessions from Yarm to South Stockton but it seems that, within a relatively short space of time, local cases had been moved to the town anyway.[340]

Despite this, Yarm had continued as a Petty Sessional Division and local cases had continued to be heard there, probably unless an appearance was urgent and/or it was more convenient to use South Stockton.[341]

Possibly because of this, the station had continued as a Sergeant's posting (although without any other officers for several years). It therefore may have seemed to the Chief Constable at least, to be a good way of resolving the 'problem' of John, as Inspector 3$^{rd}$ class may have been considered little different from Sergeant.[342]

However, if he had to leave Pickering Lythe, it would probably also have suited John, as by this time John (George) was stationed in Osmotherley (in the Northallerton Division), around 12 miles south, Alfred in York would have been readily accessible by train via Northallerton as would Julia in Loftus via Middlesbrough. In addition, as he'd attended Yarm Petty Sessions when he'd been at South Stockton, John probably knew the town, including the police station, reasonably well.

Smaller than Pickering, Yarm, or Yarm-on-Tees as it was sometimes called, was situated in a loop of the river Tees, in the Langbaurgh West Division, around 16 miles north-east of Northallerton, and 8 miles south-west of Middlesbrough.

The police station was on Bentley Wynd, then a short 'pathway' running west off the main south – north High Street, which formed the spine of the town.[343] Since 1870, when the need to accommodate a second officer at the station had become apparent, an adjoining cottage, which is likely to have been John's new home, had been rented for the officer in charge.[344]

Presumably, as they hadn't had the opportunity before John left Pickering, in April 1877, a John Hall and others from the town visited John to present him with £50 and an 'illuminated' address, in recognition of his service.[345]

The only incident reported from Yarm during the period that John was stationed there was an attempted suicide in October 1877.[346] A 16 year old servant threw herself into the Tees but was rescued and taken to Bentley Wynd, where she was charged. In the absence of any surety as to her future behaviour she was remanded before being gaoled for a month at the Quarter Sessions.[347]

Later in October the well known annual Yarm fair was held, with sales of horses on the Thursday, cattle on the Friday and sheep and lambs on the Saturday, while the concurrent cheese fair, also held in the disproportionately wide High Street, attracted further visitors.[348]

In March 1878 John was paid the equivalent of £93 16s 10d (£93.84) per annum, significantly less than if he'd continued as a Superintendent. However, at Easter he began to receive his pension (of £61 17s annually), retiring on 30 June 1878, on grounds of infirmity.[349]

Although by this time John was probably 60, his retirement may have been for other reasons. After 20 years in charge of a Division, life in Yarm may have seemed anti-climactic and unexciting, John may have simply felt that he'd had enough and/or may have been finding life as a widower difficult. Alternatively, the Chief Constable may (not necessarily ungenerously) have felt that it was time for John to finish (as it's also possible that he may have been unable to 'cope' at Yarm).

Just as when he'd moved from Essex, the force John was leaving was very different to that he'd joined 21 years and 7 months earlier. From a never actually deployed number of 50, there was now around 200 in the North Riding Constabulary.[350]

As John would have had to leave police accommodation when he retired it doesn't seem unreasonable to believe that he probably moved directly to Loftus, where his daughter and her husband would have been able to help him find a new home. Loftus was around a mile and a half from the coast and 16 miles east, south-east of Middlesbrough. Although some development had taken place on either side of the main west – east route which passed through the small market town, mostly it had been of a linear nature, with the retail and employment area at the western end and a mainly residential area, known as East Loftus, at the eastern.[351]

It was here that John was living in April 1881, although the small house on East Crescent was also occupied by Catherine (Emma) Abbot, a daughter of Jane Abbott, nee Deacon, one of Eleanor Jonas's younger sisters.

Catherine was working as a housekeeper and although she could have been employed elsewhere, domestic servants invariably 'lived in' so it's probable that she was the housekeeper for John.[352]

While it doesn't seem unreasonable that one of his sister in law's daughters may have been performing roles which his wife had undertaken in the past this, together with their family connection, may have made it difficult to maintain the usual formalities of an employer - employee relationship.

The situation may have already led to some degree of familiarity and could be connected with John giving his age at the Census as 59 (when he was probably around 63) although Catherine similarly seems to have lost a few years, being recorded as 27.[353]

Infirmity might have been given as the reason for John's retirement but, as he was to live for some time, that may have been for the benefit of the Police Committee which had to agree to any pension being paid, and it seems reasonable to believe that he was far from that condition.³⁵⁴ If anything, his health was probably reasonably robust which, together with an absence of intimate female company for some time, may have been a key factor in the relationship between John and Catherine becoming personal. When the inevitable happened, marriage was probably unavoidable, although they would have had to keep their family relationship confidential.³⁵⁵

As at least the Census enumerator would have known of this they may have left Loftus before Catherine's pregnancy became apparent, which might explain why the venue for their September 1881 wedding was Selby Register Office, although it seems unlikely that they were living in the town.³⁵⁶ As well as probably being a location where nobody knew them, by this time Selby was on the main railway line between York and the south (Doncaster), so it's possible that John and Catherine used it en-route, when visiting their respective mothers and extended families, or on their return.³⁵⁷ The latter possibility might be surprising but it seems likely that they were planning to at least stay, if not live, in Pickering.

For John, the town was somewhere he would have reasonably believed that he had many friends, and was held in some esteem, while he might have thought that he'd be isolated and lack status elsewhere. He may also have thought that there was some potential for a business in the growing tourist market, with excursion trains being operated at almost every opportunity (fairs, races etc.) and even local guide books being published.³⁵⁸

The imminent (May 1882) opening of the direct route between Scarborough and Pickering was expected to attract even more visitors.[359]

However John's former position had set him apart from most fellow citizens and it would be surprising if he didn't expect antipathy from some, particularly those he'd encountered in his 'official' capacity. Animosity might also have been anticipated as, despite the circumstances, he'd replaced his possibly well respected wife, and with a significantly younger one. Not only that, but Catherine, like Eleanor before her, would also have been a 'foreigner' with a Suffolk accent and Suffolk 'ways'.

On the other hand, an advantage of Pickering was that, although John might be well known, it was probably easier to keep their family relationship secret there than in a location they both knew better.

The town was also a reasonable location for John to access John (George) and his family, now in Thirsk, Alfred and his family in York and a railway line being built from Whitby to Loftus (for Julia and her family) would soon make the latter even more accessible.[360]

The birth of their daughter Violet (Kathleen) in Pickering, in January 1882, and the likelihood that they would have wanted Catherine to have 'settled in' before the birth, particularly as it was her first child, also suggests that they may have been en route to Pickering when they married.[361]

Further evidence that their plans were to remain in Pickering for the long term is John being reported as an executor (of a Will), in December, for a William Kneeshaw.[362]

We don't know if John had visited Pickering since his 'removal', more than five years previously, but there'd been some significant changes in the town.

The parish church, which John would have been very familiar with, had reopened after extensive refurbishment and the famous frescoes, discovered before that had begun, were no doubt attracting visitors.[363] The magistrates had begun pressing for improved accommodation almost concurrently with John's 'removal', a demand later combined with the need for a new police station.[364] As a result a new station and court house had opened on the corner of Kirkham Lane and Eastgate in May 1879.[365]

The Local Board, continuing their 'improvements' programme, had bought the Duchy of Lancaster's market rights and opened a new site on Eastgate for the sale of cattle and sheep, and in 1883, what was effectively the Board, was to open a produce market on Market Place.[366] A company with close connections to the Board had taken over the gas works in 1876 and, after building a facility of their own, and a reservoir, had been supplying the town with gas and water since 1877.[367] The Howe Bridge issue had finally been resolved and the road to Malton was readily useable after years of difficulties.

While John may have been considering opportunities in the tourism business or have planned to survive on his pension, we next hear of him in December 1887 when he was reported as being a tobacconist, toys and fancy goods dealer, at 9 Market Place, who'd petitioned for bankruptcy.[368] At his 'examination', he stated that he'd had in excess of £100 capital when he began his business but that poor trade, the high cost of borrowing, and illness had caused his insolvency.[369]

At a subsequent hearing the Official Receiver asked for £20 from John's police pension, annually for five years, although eventually £15 was agreed.[370]

Obviously John's business would have closed and it seems likely, with the significant reduction in their income, that the family left Pickering, possibly as early as spring 1888. Although we don't know where they relocated, it doesn't seem unreasonable to believe that it was Stansted (Mountfitchet), where they were living at the Census in 1891, close, and possibly even next door, to John's eldest daughter Eleanor, and her husband George Phillips.

This location isn't surprising given that it was an area that John knew, was reasonably close to their families in Lavenham and Hadleigh, and there may have been an opportunity to supplement their income, through employment of some type in George's bakery business.

They remained at the same location in 1901.

John died, aged 79, on 13 April 1903.[371]

## NOTES

1 Wool combing involved cleaning and preparing wool for spinning. After removing anything which could impede combing, the wool was cleaned, and pulled repeatedly between heated steel combs to produce thread like fibres. Combers were paid by volume and in the first half of the 19th century typically earned from 16 to 20s (shillings) (80p - £1) per week, making it a reasonably well rewarded occupation compared with, for example, agriculture were the pay for a labourer in west Suffolk could be as little as 6s (30p) a week during particularly depressed times (Philips & Storch p193).

2 John was probably born around the time that Charles and Ann married, as during this period baptism typically occurred within a few weeks of a birth. The marriage therefore probably occurred relatively 'late', when in normal circumstances at least the potential bride would have been aware of a pregnancy and usually, arrangements made for a marriage as soon as possible* (assuming that the potential bridegroom was willing and able). In this case a 'late' marriage might suggest that Charles was either not available earlier for some reason, or not the original potential bridegroom (because he wasn't John's father). Further evidence for the latter contention is that the marriage doesn't seem to have led to any other children, when the typical number of births around this time was between four and five (Speigelhalter p170 & 175). If Ann wouldn't or couldn't name a father who would take (financial) responsibility for his child, as the prevailing Poor Laws required, she would have been increasingly anxious to find a husband. Despite Charles being younger, possibly 23, when she was probably 26, she may have accepted any proposal that he might have made, which for him at least provided the status (and benefits) of husband.

*Harrison p84: brides being pregnant was considered an almost universal occurrence among Ann's age group, in rural areas during this period.

3 As well as giving his father's name as Emanuel, John also gave his occupation as wool merchant.

Although there may have been others, and the Census was more than 20 years later, the only Emanuel recorded in Lavenham in 1841 was Emmanuel How, or Howe, who was a wool comber. However, he may also have been regarded as a wool merchant as self employed combers would often have bought and sold wool.

Intriguingly, he'd married John's paternal aunt Eliza in November 1820, so it's possible that he might have had a relationship with the then Ann Gooch at least three years earlier, which led to her pregnancy but for some reason, didn't lead to their marriage. On the other hand, John may simply have been acknowledging a role that Emanuel had played in his life - Eliza and Charles Jonas were 'close' – she was a witness at the wedding of her nearest born sibling.

[4] In July 1831 the *Bury & Norwich Post* reported a theft from Charles Jonas (the only identifiable one in the area) of Preston, which is where he and Ann were living in 1841, 1851 and 1861.

[5] The 1841 Census recorded a population of 406 – more than half of those with an occupation were Agricultural Labourers.

[6] Although some, from both families, may have moved elsewhere by then, in 1841 John's paternal grandparents were living on High Street, a maternal aunt and her family on Market Place and paternal aunt Eliza and family on Bolton Street.

[7] Yorke p26 & 107

Furniture was probably limited to a table with chairs and a couple of metal framed beds with straw filled mattresses. The floor would probably have been compressed earth (Harrison p71) or stone slabs, possibly supplemented by string or rag rugs. It's unlikely that there would have been any decoration.

Water could be boiled, and simple dishes such as porridge, stews and soups cooked using an open fire, although the family may have had a simple hob arrangement. They probably also cooked other steamed foods, such as dumplings and suet puddings, but otherwise meals probably consisted of little more than bread, cheese and potatoes. Occasionally they may have had meat, although this would usually have been limited to offal, or pork in one form or another, particularly bacon. For special occasions there might have been a home reared pig or chicken, or a locally caught rabbit or hare (although penalties for poaching, if that was involved, were severe).

[8] Using older children ('monitors') to teach younger ones in an inexpensive, basic education system, the *British (and Foreign School) Society)* was *(for the Education of the Labouring and Manufacturing Classes of Society of Every Religious Persuasion*) while the *National (Society)* was *(for Promoting the Education of the Poor in the Principle of the Established Church)*.

⁹ Adult ages were supposed to be 'rounded' down to the nearest number divisible by five for the 1841 Census (although this wasn't applied consistently) so John's age was recorded as 20.

¹⁰ As a John Ranson had been a witness at the marriage of Charles and Ann, with a Sarah (probably John Ranson's wife) later performing the same function for John Jonas, it wouldn't be surprising if John's apprenticeship was to an Isaac Ranson (probably one of their sons), shoemaker of Bolton Street.

¹¹ One of the witnesses at the marriage of their oldest surviving daughter was a John Deacon. The only John Deacon this was likely to have been, who was included in the 1841 Census at Lavenham, had his place of birth recorded as Ireland. In 1891 his age was recorded as 78 and his place of birth as Co. Kilkenny. The latter, and a probable birth year of 1812, which is consistent with the subsequent pattern of births in the family, suggest that John was Robert and Eleanor's first child and that they'd married (and therefore probably met) in Ireland, before he was born.

¹² If he was her brother, Eleanor was the second oldest surviving child after John Deacon – their closest sibling was born in Lavenham, probably early in 1814, but died in infancy.

¹³ 'Tinkers', who were often itinerant, mended (cooking) pots, pans, utensils and the like.

¹⁴ The 2 or 3d* it typically cost for a week of school (Best p174), was a relatively large sum when the average weekly Deacon family income was probably little different from that of an agricultural labourer. However, children didn't necessarily attend school every day – if money was limited, or paid work was available, they were likely to be absented.

Eleanor's probable lack of education is evident from her being unable to write her name when registering a birth in 1840 – around half of females were literate at this time (two thirds of males) (Walvin p94 & Harrison p135). Although she supposedly signed the Register when she married (as it wasn't 'marked'), that could have been done on her behalf (possibly by her husband).

* Derived from the Latin *denarius* or *denarii,* d was the symbol for pre decimal pennies, which were each worth slightly less than ½p, so 2 or 3d was worth around 1p.

[15] As we only have their respective baptism dates we can't be certain of the age difference between them, but John may have been around two years younger than Eleanor, a difference which can seem significant at that age (and might suggest that they 'had' to get married).

[16] The civil registration of births, deaths and marriages didn't begin until mid 1837 and it was some time before it became universal, particularly in the case of births.
Despite places of birth given at later Censuses it's unlikely that Eleanor or John were born somewhere other than Lavenham as that would probably have been recorded in the Church Register.

[17] It seems reasonable to believe, based on later Census information, that Eleanor was born in 1836 and John in 1837.

[18] If there were fears for the life of a child, baptism might be arranged within days of birth (as un-baptised dead could not be buried in consecrated ground).

[19] Harrison p24: the depression was at its worst during the 1837 – 1842 period.

[20] John's apprenticeship would have finished when he was 21 (Pringle p157), soon after which (autumn 1839) Eleanor's third pregnancy might have begun to become an issue.

[21] Best p31: the 'usual' migration distance averaged 10 miles although some people successively repeated this over time.

[22] While it could have been some form of lodging house, or premises let room by room, it's possible that Carmen's Buildings was a 'court' arrangement. These were generally created by using undeveloped space behind the properties which otherwise lined a street, and by their nature offered very limited accommodation. The 'houses' in such 'courts', each sometimes consisting of no more than a couple of rooms, were generally clustered around some sort of central communal area which might be enclosed or, more typically was open to the environment. The communal area probably accommodated a widely shared 'privy', and 'drinking' water may have been available from a standpipe although might have had to be brought from a pump in a nearby street. 'Courts' were notorious for their lack of ventilation and daylight, and generally insanitary conditions (Best p38).
At the time of the Census John was almost 12 miles north at Marsham, Norfolk (presumably seeking orders for shoes).

[23] Historically, Boroughs were towns or cities which had been given special 'privileges' (generally by the monarch), such as the rights to hold (revenue raising and trade generating) markets and to levy (local taxes) rates. Their status made them independent from the counties which they were geographically part of and they were governed by separate administrations.

As well as providing a standardised framework for the government of Boroughs, the 1835 Municipal Corporations Act authorised the establishment of Borough police forces.

Pursuing a Charter of political rights, the Chartists formed a mass working class movement which was perceived as a threat to the government (Cowley p53). However, while the latter may have been concerned by the movement and used it to introduce legislation (Philips & Storch p138), the generally inconsistent adoption of the 1839 Rural Constabulary Act suggests that Chartism wasn't the key motivator in many counties (Taylor p28 & 29). In the case of Essex for example it may have been serious outbreaks of disorder earlier in the century which produced support for a county Constabulary (Rawlings p135).

Whatever their motivation, the 1839 Act permitted Justices (of the Peace) (magistrates) to appoint Chief Constables for the direction of police in their areas, allowing a maximum of one officer per 1,000 population. As a result, among others, Essex and Norfolk Constabularies were constituted in November 1839 (and East Suffolk in March 1840) (Cowley p62).

[24] Philips & Storch p193: the Lighting and Watching Act had been designed to allow parishes or small towns to provide policing. Such arrangements were absorbed into county forces under the 1839 Act and the supplementary 1840 County Police Act (Philips & Storch p216).

[25] Captain (Capt.) McHardy, the Chief Constable of Essex, later (*Chelmsford Chronicle* October 1850) contended that recruits were attracted, generally by the incremental pay scale and prospects of promotion, and particularly by the permanency of the positions and of the salaries.

[26] West Suffolk wasn't constituted until January 1845 (Cowley p62) and in Norfolk (Butcher p16) a potential candidate described the height requirement as near 6' (1.83m).

123

[27] The Sudbury force had been formed in 1835 (Cowley p43). Although the government's aim in authorising their establishment might have been to emulate the, by then, generally acclaimed Metropolitan Police, most of the Borough forces were small, offered limited opportunities and lacked 'professionalism'. They were usually operated with insufficient funding, often suffered from political interference and generally didn't bear comparison with the county forces until coerced, after later legislation.

[28] The national average male height at the time was 5'6" (1.68m) (Pritchard p150).

[29] The entrance requirements, which also applied to Superintendents, were in the *Rules*, produced on behalf of the Home Secretary, Lord Normanby, for mandatory application (*Essex Standard* October 1839) by the Quarter Sessions magistrates and their Chief Constables, as they organised the new police forces. Unsurprisingly the *Rules* were based on Metropolitan Police experience (Critchley p52, 87 & 88).

[30] Woodgate p11: although April - August inclusive were particularly busy, there wasn't any month (*General Force Register* - ERO J/P 2/1) in 1842 in which men weren't sworn in. When the incidence of the oath being given coincided with a meeting of the Quarter Sessions\* (in the Shire Hall, Chelmsford) then it's likely that the event occurred in their presence. Otherwise, and as the procedure was sometimes required several times in a month, it seems probable that the Chief Constable and/or Clerk (of the Peace) and/or a few local magistrates, would have officiated on most occasions, such as when John, together with five other recruits, gave his oath.

\*As well as forming a court, the Quarter Sessions, named because they were held on, or close to the traditional 'quarter' days of the year – Epiphany (January), Lent or Easter (April), Midsummer (July) and Michaelmas (September), also provided the only tier of government which existed at this time between the centre in London and the parish locally. Made up of the (Crown appointed) magistrates from across the area, such as the county, over which their Sessions had jurisdiction, before 'sitting' as a court they discussed and agreed policy in regard to their other responsibilities. These included gaols, lunatic asylums and facilities such as lock ups and bridges.

The rates (local taxes) to pay for these were generally set by Finance Committees and those Sessions which had implemented the 1839 Act also had Police or Constabulary Committees. The latter, a requirement of the Act, presented quarterly reports (as did the Chief Constable) which covered all aspects of police operations, including buildings and manpower.

[31] The force also included twenty Inspectors and fifteen Superintendents: *Return of the Distribution of the Essex County Constabulary* presented to Quarter Sessions (*Chelmsford Chronicle* April 1842).

[32] *General Force Register* - ERO J/P 2/1

[33] Woodgate p11 & 12: 'guard' was a term that Capt. McHardy had brought from H.M. Coastguard (where he'd spent the last nine years of his career before becoming Chief Constable).

The concept of patrolling (to prevent crime), and on a regulated pattern and frequency, was one of several significant differences between the police forces initiated from 1829 and the arrangements, or often lack of them, which prevailed before then.

[34] There were however a further two Inspectors and six Constables (the number varied slightly each month) elsewhere in the Chelmsford Division (*Essex Standard* April 1842).

[35] In April 1839 the then Home Secretary asked the Commissioners of the Metropolitan Police to draft the first (county) constabulary rules (Critchley p87). These were presumably what Lord Normanby was referring to in a letter, presented to the Quarter Sessions in November 1839 (*Essex Standard*), which mentioned him sending a copy to them of a >summary (as soon as it was completed) of the instructions and guidance respecting the duties and powers of Constables. It seems likely that this was what was later forwarded to the counties as *Instructions Respecting the Duties and Powers of Constables* (GA Q/AP/3) with the intention that Chief Constables, in adherence to Normanby's *Rules*, used it to produce guidance for their Constables and Superintendents (initially there were no other ranks in the provincial forces).

These *Instructions* were probably extracted from, or a copy of, the 1829 Metropolitan Police *Instructions* (*General Instructions for the different ranks of the Police Force*) (Metropolitan Police Heritage Centre). →

Although the latter covered ranks (Inspectors and Sergeants) which didn't exist in Essex, described the structure of a force many times larger and how it was to operate in a mainly urban environment and included a considerable number of metropolis specific rules, slightly more than half of the *General Instructions* were potentially applicable anywhere. It isn't surprising therefore that Capt. McHardy used almost all of the latter content in his *Orders and Instructions Framed and Issued for the Superintendents and Constables of the Essex Constabulary*. However, the Metropolitan Police material only constituted slightly more than half of the latter (even excluding Capt. McHardy's forms/returns), as the Chief Constable and probably the Clerk* (of the Peace) added other guidance, such as action to be taken in the event of a robbery. Capt. McHardy also included a considerable number of, what can only be described as, 'administrative' instructions, such as how officers' *Journals* were to be completed.

The Chief Constable presented his *Orders and ...* to the April 1840 Quarter Sessions (*Chelmsford Chronicle*) for approval before a copy was sent to the Home Office, for concurrence.

(A revised version was issued in 1849 and another was published, on the basis of a date included among the text, probably sometime during 1859.)

The day to day 'guidance' contained in *Orders and ...* was another significant innovation of 'new' policing (Melville Lee p298 & 299).

*The Clerk (of the Peace), appointed to the Quarter Sessions, was usually a member of the legal profession (typically a local solicitor), who would have been able to contribute his knowledge and experience of how law enforcement operated in the area and therefore what might have been considered essential for inclusion in the Chief Constable's *Orders and ...* .

[36] The uniform and equipment issued was stipulated in Normanby's *Rules* – in Essex the 'tail' coat was replaced by the popular (Goodman p44) 'frock' style, in 1855. The great coats were the same as those worn by the Metropolitan Police and (together with the capes) were probably made of tightly woven wool, impervious to wind and rain (Goodman p42). The hats were re-enforced with stiff leather, and later a wire and cane or wooden frame, for protection and to enable them to be stood on to look over hedges and walls.

'Top' hats were the most popular general form of headwear at the time (Goodman p54, 58 & 59).

[37] *Orders and ...*

[38] Woodgate p14: for Constable 2$^{nd}$ class the rate was 19s (95p) per week and for Constable 1$^{st}$ class 21s (£1.05).

[39] 1849 *Orders and ...* Appendix: Halstead police district population 5,595.

[40] In Essex (and in some other counties), as the ancient 'Hundreds' (by then based on ecclesiastical parishes) often already defined the jurisdiction areas of the existing law enforcement structures they tended to be used, although often reconfigured, as the basis for the new police Divisions.

[41] Halstead police station, created in 1841 in the town's 'House of Correction' through moving the prisoners held there to Chelmsford, was on Bridge Street, which linked High Street and Trinity Street, at the bottom of the river valley. At the least it would have consisted of several cells and a charge room. Some stations also had what were sometimes described as 'guard rooms' (where officers assembled) as well as day, cleaning and rest rooms and 'airing' yards for prisoners to 'exercise'.

[42] Essentially equivalent to the contemporary Magistrates Court, the Petty Sessions, or Police Court, operated daily, weekly, fortnightly or monthly, depending on when, and how many, cases required hearing. Typically, up to three magistrates 'sat', without a jury, and sentenced those they found guilty to minor punishments of fines and/or costs, or jail for between a few days and several weeks. If the seriousness of an offence warranted a more significant penalty the accused were committed to the Quarter Sessions, where typically three magistrates 'sat' with a jury. Quarter Sessions could pass sentences of up to seven years (penal servitude) but more serious, and certainly capital offences, which carried the death penalty, were sent to the Assizes. The latter were usually held twice a year in Spring (Lent) and Summer although if the need arose a third Assizes (sometimes called a 'Gaol Delivery') was held in the Winter (December). In Essex the Assizes, presided over by a visiting 'professional' judge, were also held in the Shire Hall, Chelmsford.

Variations of this structure applied in the Boroughs and in the Metropolitan Police area.

⁴³ *Orders and ...* set down how patrols were to be performed - it seems probable that the route of a 'guard' passed at least every occupied, if not all premises within the area involved. Constables were expected to cover all of their 'guard' but were empowered to make variations if they had good reasons for doing so. The route and key places to be checked on each 'guard' were noted on cards which were supplied to the Constable carrying out the patrol, who also had to personally acquaint himself with every resident on the route.

Details of the 'guards' had to be kept confidential but the idea of fixed routes, which potential law breakers might identify and take 'advantage' of, seems strange in current times. However, a set route for a 'guard' meant that the public would know where and when they'd next see a Constable, or find one, and that Constables could develop relationships with those on their routes. In this way they were more likely to pick up local intelligence which was critical as, to paraphrase a section in the 1849 version of *Orders and ...* , nine out of ten criminals lived in the neighbourhood of, or seldom more than a few miles from the place where their crimes were committed.

Officers from different 'guards' (sometimes from different districts and/or Divisions) were also expected to meet (at locations specified on the card used to detail the 'guard'), 'confer' and patrol together.

⁴⁴ Best p88: unless roads were turnpiked or tolled (generally only 'main' routes), they were usually little more than worn tracks over uncultivated ground. Close to towns they might have had some stones, chippings or gravel spread across them but probably little, or nothing more was done otherwise. Muddy and flooded in winter, dusty and rutted in summer, it was the failure of local citizens to carry out repairs, and the reluctance of local ratepayers to meet the costs, which had led to the creation of toll or turnpiked roads, although acquiring that status didn't guarantee improvement.

⁴⁵ Woodgate p16: the lamps had a spring clip on the back so they could be attached to a Constable's belt, or a handle could be unfolded and the lamp carried to illuminate suspects or crime scenes. The lens could be readily covered, enabling the lamp to be kept alight throughout a patrol without indicating an officers' presence.

[46] *Essex Standard* May 1843
[47] *General Force Register* - ERO J/P 2/1
[48] *Police Force Distribution* - ERO Q/APr 2
[49] Initially, for example, an Inspector was stationed at Foxearth (together with a Constable) but the post ceased from June 1843 (*Police Force Distribution* - ERO Q/APr 2).
[50] Walvin p167
[51] The birth of a child wasn't an opportunity for paternal leave but Constables could have a week of unpaid holiday each year (Woodgate p14).
[52] 1849 *Orders and* ... Appendix: population of Foxearth 474.
Mention of a police station in a *Bury and Norwich Post* report in January 1844 suggests that there may have been some sort of structure in Foxearth but, if anything existed, it was unlikely to have been more than a lock up and as these were primarily cages (for holding prisoners) the accommodation they provided was usually limited. It's probable that any such structure would have been the product of Capt. McHardy's programme (*Orders and* ...) to provide short term holding facilities around the county. Otherwise, anything which had existed before the force was established would have made it likely that Foxearth would have been a 'station' from that time, as it would have been difficult to overlook, given that the Police Committee, charged with establishing the Constabulary, had specifically instructed the Chief Constable (*Essex Standard* April 1840) to investigate potential locations for police stations and lock ups.
Although Constables could also be located in other premises previously used by parish constables, or in a gaol such as at Halstead, an alternative explanation is that 'station' signified nothing more than a locality to which a Constable was assigned (or in some counties, where he lived). Perhaps, it was to avoid the potential for confusion that sometimes 'house', or a similar suffix, was appended to 'station' to indicate a building.
[53] *Chelmsford Chronicle* March 1845 & *Essex Standard* October 1847
[54] *Bury and Norwich Post* January 1848
The Petty Sessions were held at the Bell inn, Castle Hedingham, until 1852 (Pawsey p37).
[55] *Chelmsford Chronicle* February 1848
[56] *Police Force Distribution* - ERO Q/APr 7

[57] 1859 *Orders and* ... Appendix: population of Sible Hedingham 2,346.
[58] Woodgate p27: the building, which was later extended to accommodate Castle Hedingham Petty Sessions, which moved there in 1852, is now a private residence (Pawsey p37 & 38).
[59] The role of assistant Relieving Officer involved questioning vagrants, particularly in regard to their origins and why they shouldn't return to them. Otherwise, according to the Chief Constable (*Chelmsford Chronicle* October & November 1853), the process involved searching the vagrants and logging their details and full descriptions. Following this, the records of those provided with, and those denied relief (with the reasons for refusal), would have been checked for previous applications. If considered 'deserving', applicants would be given a 'ticket' of admission (to the Workhouse*), although anything of value found on them was used to offset the cost of this. The 'undeserving', usually 'professional' vagrants, would be rejected, although according to Capt. McHardy, their dislike of police examination might have already deterred them and was sufficient to deter them in the future.
At the same time as they began this role, Essex Constabulary also seems to have begun inspecting lodging houses *(Chelmsford Chronicle* October 1848 & Melville Lee p303).
* Workhouses, often provided by 'Unions' of parishes acting together, provided rudimentary accommodation for the poor and needy.
[60] Unsurprisingly more than half of the substantive section (excluding the Appendix, Forms and Returns, and Index) of *Orders and Instructions Framed and Issued for the Government of the Essex Constabulary* was copied from the 1840 version.
This included all of the content drawn from the 1829 Metropolitan Police *General Instructions* and most of the locally generated material which had been added to that, although changing circumstances and the benefit of experience probably accounted for around a tenth which wasn't carried forward.
(White) summer trousers were no longer required but officers obviously needed more guidance when dealing with robberies or livestock thefts.

There were instructions regarding weights and measures, controlling public houses, handling prisoners, using warrants, giving evidence and signing depositions; terms and conditions sections included superannuation deductions and good conduct awards.

[61] *Chelmsford Chronicle* August & October 1849

[62] Although the latest version of *Orders and ...* included detailed instructions regarding footmarks [*sic*], these didn't extend to taking impressions using plaster of paris in a practice which had been employed elsewhere for some time (Lock p148 & 149).

[63] *Essex Standard* April 1850

[64] Constables could apply to become 2nd class after six months and 1st class after a further eighteen months (Woodgate p14). However, while this might have been a guiding principle and/or an assumption used in calculating the future cost of the Constabulary, it isn't what always seems to have happened in practice. For example, of nineteen recruits, from the period between March 1840 and October 1844, whose careers can be readily tracked through the *General Force Register* (ERO J/P 2/1), although two were soon promoted to Constable 1st class, the remainder waited an average seven years and two months to be promoted to 2nd class and a further fourteen years and two months to become 1st class – fourteen survived to collect superannuation.

[65] John's lack of promotion can't have been due to a shortage of vacancies – 80% of 150 men recruited as Constables, 1840 – 45, left within an average of 26 months. The reasons for leaving weren't usually recorded in the *General Force Register* in this period and there has to be some doubt regarding the real level of dismissals (only fifty nine were documented as dismissed/ discharged/permitted to resign), as resignations may have been considered (politically) preferable.

It seems far more likely therefore that the reason for John not being promoted was the episode involving escapees in Halstead* and/or the relationship he'd had with his Divisional Superintendent, who'd been an Inspector at Foxearth before promotion to Superintendent at (Great Bardfield in February 1843 and) Castle Hedingham in December 1843 (ERO Q/Apr 2 & 3).

*There may have been some suspicion that John hadn't checked his prisoners as frequently as was expected, allowing them time to make the hole in the cell wall and escape.

The episode would have been at least embarrassing for the Chief Constable and may, to use a contemporary term, have brought the force 'into disrepute'.

[66] The Inquest reached a verdict of accidental death through gunshot. The autopsy doctor reported that after Poole's death he'd extracted several pieces of shot from the latter's arm. As all were flattened, but only some against bone, he suggested that this had probably been because they'd passed through Flower's arm before entering Poole.

[67] As *Orders and* ... forbade officers from taking money from anyone, on any occasion, this would have required the express permission of the Chief Constable.

[68] Transportation was curtailed from 1853 by the Penal Servitude Act of that year and theoretically abolished by a further Act in 1857, but continued until 1867. It's been estimated that more than 140,000 men, women and children were transported to Australia (and Tasmania), the destination(s) then in use - the majority for theft (Harrison p62).

[69] *Bury and Norwich Post* & *Essex Standard* June & July 1851

[70] *Essex Standard*

[71] As with Constables, the different classes of Inspector had been introduced to limit salary costs.

John was the last of nine from the 1842 intake (waiting an average four years and two months) who became Inspectors (His promotion coincided with the resignation of his Divisional Superintendent (effective from 31 December 1852).

Initially Essex didn't have any rank between Superintendent and Constable, but at the October 1840 Quarter Sessions, Capt. McHardy had received approval to appoint Inspectors to improve the supervision of the Constables, as well as to represent Superintendents when they were away from their Divisions (*Chelmsford Chronicle*). Although some counties introduced Sergeants rather than Inspectors, at least for the former role, Capt. McHardy considered Inspector a better job title than Sergeant. As a result, it was 1855 (Woodgate p13) before the Chief Constable sought authority to convert some Inspectors' posts to Sergeants' (partly because he couldn't recruit sufficient and partly as an economy measure), providing Essex with a further intermediate grade.

When John was promoted, the number of Inspectors on the Establishment was twenty but this was halved when the ten Sergeants' posts were created. The pay for the latter was midway between Constable 1$^{st}$ class and Inspector 3$^{rd}$ class, which may have presented some incentive to those seeking advancement, as McHardy hoped, but at the same time reducing the number of Inspectors and of Superintendents (fifteen to ten as part of the same re-organisation) might have had the opposite effect (*Essex Standard* October 1854).

[72] *Police Force Distribution* - ERO Q/APr 9

[73] Canals were also used to move goods but didn't have the geographical coverage of roads (and railways) and tended to be concentrated in industrial areas. In East Anglia several rivers were navigable and used in a similar way as canals.

[74] 1859 *Orders and* ... Appendix: population of Southminster 1,482.

[75] Scollan p10 & 11

[76] Woodgate p28

[77] Smith p109, 127 & 128

The Chief Constable however, possibly for 'political' (and/or 'nostalgic') reasons, seems to have continued to regard smuggling as a significant issue.

[78] Capt. McHardy had told an 1853 (House of) Commons Select Committee that 127 H.M. Coastguard staff were stationed on the Essex coast (*Chelmsford Chronicle* October & November 1853).

[79] *Chelmsford Chronicle* January 1853: the 1840 County Police Act enabled private individuals and/or organisations to fund additional Constables (Critchley p91 & Steadman p45). Several, including an Inspector, had been employed since 1848 by the Burnham Oyster Company (Woodgate p35 & ERO Q/Apr 6) although a county funded Constable continued to also be stationed in the town.

[80] Ironically, while two Constables had originally been stationed there, by January 1842 (*Essex Standard*) one of those posts had been uprated to Inspector and by October 1842 (*Essex Standard*) that was the only post remaining, which meant that John had no alternative to patrolling the town himself.

*Police Force Distribution* - ERO A/Ppr 9 & 10

[81] *Chelmsford Chronicle* April 1840 & *Orders and* ...

[82] Scollan p12

[83] Woodgate p14

133

[84] Among other information, the *Police Gazette* provided details, including descriptions, of wanted persons and stolen property.
[85] Scollan p20: Essex Constabulary had been undertaking the role of Weights and Measures Inspectors since 1843.
[86] *Circulars issued by the Chief Constable to Superintendents* - ERO Q/APp 5
[87] *Chelmsford Chronicle* June 1853 & *Essex Standard* July 1853: Asheldham
*Essex Standard* January & April 1854: Tillingham
[88] *Essex Standard* & *Chelmsford Chronicle* October 1854
[89] *1859 Orders and* ... Appendix: population of Stansted Mountfitchet 1,719.
[90] With no viable alternative, railways were extremely important at this time, providing the general population with mobility over distance, in a practical timespan, at a relatively affordable cost.
[91] The type of accommodation which the family might have aspired to would possibly have included a kitchen with a cooking range on which a relatively wider variety of foods could be prepared. Two types of range, both wood or coal fuelled, were in use at this time (Goodman p159). The original arrangement had essentially been an open fire, with metal boxes on either side, which could be used for a variety of purposes, but this was increasingly replaced by what we think of as a Victorian range. This had an enclosed fire, with an oven on one side, and a second oven, or water boiler, on the other. Above these was a cooking surface for pots, pans, kettles and the like. The family might also have sought a living room, and possibly three bedrooms, so the two sons could be separated from their two sisters, although other facilities such as a bathroom, toilet or piped water would almost certainly not have been available. They probably would have also expected more furniture and decoration, and even partially carpeted floors.
[92] Although not directly comparable, as the information is from different sources and different years, an analysis of Indictable Offences* in 1854 indicates that in terms of number per 1,000 population** Walden suffered a similar incidence (2.9) as Dengie (2.8) and North Hinckford (2.7) with South Hinckford, which included the larger towns of Braintree/Bocking and Halstead, significantly higher (4.6).

A greater divergence existed in terms of number of Offences per officer in each Division***, from 2.54 in Dengie to 6.50 in South Hinckford via 3.86 and 4.20 in Walden and North Hinckford respectively. This meant that on average, officer Jonas would have had to contend with one Indictable Offence every eight weeks in Halstead, twelve in Foxearth/Sible Hedingham, twenty in Southminster and thirteen in Stansted (Mountfitchet). This makes it likely that John's time would have mostly been spent dealing with minor offences (which fell within the jurisdiction of Petty Sessions) and for patrolling.

*Essentially those which warranted sentencing at Quarter Sessions or Assizes, the major (93%) Indictable Offence (ERO Q/App 5) in Essex was Larceny, in its many forms, with Arson and Forgery the only other significant, but relatively minor categorisations (2.4% and 1.7% respectively).

**The populations used are those in the Appendix of the 1849 *Orders and ...* which are likely to have been based on the 1841 Census – the populations in the Appendix of the 1859 *Orders and ...* aren't comparable as they relate to the different Divisions by then in place.

***The number of officers in each Division is from a Return published in the *Chelmsford Chronicle* in December 1853, although numbers altered little over the next few years (ERO Q/Apr 10).

[93] The Saffron Walden Petty Sessions (and Borough Quarter Sessions) 'sat' at the Town Hall (Woodgate p169) and dealt with county, as well as Borough cases, (*Essex Standard* September 1853 & January 1855) while a police or magistrates court, handling county cases, sometimes 'sat' at Newport. The Saffron Walden Borough force, formed in 1835 (Cowley p42), had an Inspector and four Constables (1859 *Orders and ...* Appendix).

[94] A 'station' was mentioned in a case reported by the *Chelmsford Chronicle* in November 1855 but the reference may have been made in the same way as that for Foxearth (see above).

[95] *Police Force Distribution* - ERO Q/Apr 9/10

[96] The type of clock with sufficient space to hide items would almost certainly have been what is often referred to as long case or 'grandfather'.

[97] *Essex Standard* January & *Chelmsford Chronicle* March 1855

[98] *Essex Standard* January & February 1855

[99] The telegraph was a pre telephone communication system – it worked by sending electrical pulses between two 'instruments', each capable of creating the pulses and turning them (with further processing) into meaningful text. The police had employed the system as early as 1841 (Melville Lee p364), but it increased in use significantly after the establishment of the *Electric Telegraph Company* in 1846 (Simmons p226), with many instruments being installed in post offices throughout the country.

[100] *Cambridge Independent Press* June & *Hertfordshire Guardian* July 1855

[101] *Chelmsford Chronicle* November 1855
*Process Book of Indictments* – ERO Q/SPb

[102] *Essex Standard* May 1856

[103] It isn't surprising that the North Riding was at the forefront. In the past the county had recognised a need for, and supported the principles behind, 'new' policing (Philips & Storch p137 & 236), and had considered forming a force under the 1839 Act (Philips & Storch p158). Now, as well as having the benefit of the experience of counties which had taken that initiative, there was no longer any option but to establish (and pay) for a county wide police structure.

[104] Critchley p107

[105] *York Herald* October 1856: Captain Hill's rank was military - he'd served in the 24th Regiment of Foot and latterly the North York Rifles.

[106] In 1861 John Richard Hill, and a younger brother, James, were rectors (alternative to, but similar responsibilities as vicars) respectively, of Thornton (Dale) and Normanby (around 5 miles south-west of Pickering). Clergy had a disproportionate presence on local (magistrates) 'benches' in many areas – not solely Yorkshire – more than one in five of the magistrates at the election for the post of Chief Constable were clergy (*York Herald* October 1856).

The Hills (and their colleagues) probably admired the Essex Chief Constable's self-proclaimed ability to provide a 'model' service, at apparently minimal cost, possibly having read his lengthy presentation to the Commons Select Committee (*Chelmsford Chronicle* October & November 1853), when Capt. McHardy had explained in detail how his force was self-financing.

In another part of his evidence, which would have particularly appealed to members of the moorland agricultural communities, the Essex Chief Constable also claimed that his force had achieved a significant reduction in sheep stealing.

[107] *York Herald* October 1856: although there were three other candidates for the position of Chief Constable, an endorsement from the Essex post holder would have carried considerable weight, although of course it would have been surprising if Capt. Hill's brothers hadn't also lobbied strongly on his behalf – he received 85 of the 123 votes cast.

[108] Many of those from other counties who gave evidence to the Commons Select Committee had gained experience in Essex (Steadman p20), so Capt. Hill would have been aware of the potential of the county as a source of recruits.

[109] Thornton doesn't seem to have had the le prefix appended to Dale until the mid 1870s in the case of the *York Herald* and around a century later in the case of the *Ordnance Survey*. In a slightly different vein the *Herald* generally used Kirbymoorside, although occasionally that became Kirby Moorside, while the contemporary *Ordnance Survey* version was Kirkby Moorside.

[110] Steadman p22: statement
It isn't surprising that Capt. McHardy had been persuaded to 'provide' some Essex officers, given that in the past (*Chelmsford Chronicle* April 1842) he'd stated that he always aimed to fill Superintendent's posts with men who'd been in the police (or in the army).

[111] Normanby's *Rules* stipulated an upper age limit of 40 - John was probably 38 (36 was the age recorded when he started with the North Riding Constabulary – *Register of Constables* NYCRO MIC 1249 QP).
Capt. Hill was 34 that November (*York Herald* October 1856).

[112] The likelihood that while in Essex John had been designated for the post he was soon to undertake seems more certain in the light of him being one of the first Superintendents to begin with the North Riding Constabulary.

[113] Best p31

[114] When John resigned from the Essex Constabulary, Alfred and John (George) were recorded in the *General Force Register* as dependent, and probably went with their parents to Yorkshire.

137

[115] According to the 1856 – 57 annual* report of the Inspector of Constabulary (or Crown/Government Inspector as they were sometimes called), Superintendents in the North Riding were paid £100, £90 or £80 per year. By 1858 – 59 this had increased to £120, £95 or £85, plus travelling allowances.
This was significantly more than John earned as an Inspector and a relatively substantial salary when the vast majority of the population 'enjoyed' an annual income of less than £70 per year.
* The year covered October – September during this period.
Inspector of Constabulary annual reports can be viewed on the ProQuest *House of Commons Parliamentary Papers* electronic database (formerly published by Chadwyck – Healey).
[116] Putting his affairs in order included returning his uniform, and other issued 'equipment', and providing 5s (25p) to pay for the former to be altered to fit his replacement (*Orders and ...*).
[117] The background of officers wasn't as mixed as it had been in Essex – of 115 of all ranks in March 1859 there were 72 with previous police experience (*Register of Constables* - NYCRO MIC 1249 QP).
Superintendents were the immediate subordinates of the Chief Constable.
[118] The second most populated, but most economically active of the police Divisions, Langbaurgh, was split into East (Guisborough) and West (Stokesley) in 1867.
[119] Although already a long established resort, the opening of the railway from York in 1845 had been the catalyst for a relatively rapid expansion of Scarborough (Best p224). However, it wasn't only tourists, brought by the railway, which provided the challenge for the Borough force as the population (which would have been partly swollen by early season visitors) increased from almost 13,000 in 1851 (Walvin p154) to more than 17,000 in 1861, with another 5,000 by 1871 (*York Herald* April 1871). This would have made the town a very different policing prospect from Pickering Lythe and including it in the latter Division would have created a significant imbalance. It therefore doesn't seem unreasonable to believe that Scarborough would have been established as a separate Division had it not remained independent. It also seems reasonable to believe, if that had been the case, that the Division would have extended beyond the area policed by the Borough and taken in part of Pickering Lythe.

[120] NYCRO MIC 1390 – QAP
[121] Although Scalby and Cayton included considerable stretches of coastline, with the exception of Cayton Bay this essentially consisted of rocky foreshores and high cliffs so probably wouldn't have required any regular police attention.
[122] Hackness seems to have been policed as part of Pickering Lythe probably because it didn't warrant any significant and/or permanent police presence.
[123] In 1861 the populations of the town were 3,398 and of the parish 4,701, which became 3,679 and 4,963 respectively by 1871 (*York Herald* May 1871).
[124] Hayes & Ruther p7
[125] *Malton Messenger* April 1869
[126] Apart from toll bars, milestones and, in the North Riding, direction signs, nothing probably indicated the 'status' of a road, other than perhaps the condition, which probably suggested how much it was used and in what way, so travellers wouldn't have felt confined to 'designated' routes.
[127] *York Herald* June & October 1869
Although the prime aim was to maintain and increase the prosperity of Whitby, overcoming the problem of the roads being impassable was probably a major reason behind the building of the railway to Pickering, as even snow didn't prevent that operating (Bell p73).
[128] Serious flooding was reported in February 1861 (*Yorkshire Gazette*), when it was described as the fourth occasion that winter and the highest for several years. In November 1863 (*York Herald*) parts of Pickering were flooded in the most significant inundation for 18 years. Flooding in September 1866 (*York Herald*) was described as the worst in 35 years, with the lower areas of Pickering again being affected and roads made impassable. Six months later (*York Herald* February 1867) the Malton road at Howe Bridge was under 5' (1.52m) of water and the railway line to Rillington was surrounded by floods as deep as 3' (0.91m) – it was stated that a lake 30 miles long and a mile wide had been created in the vale.
[129] The Jonas's route may have been via Cambridge to Huntingdon, then to York, and from there to Pickering via Rillington. →

The line from Rillington junction to Pickering had opened on the same day as that between York and Scarborough, but passengers may have been limited until 1847 when upgrading of the Whitby & Pickering line to accommodate steam haulage (it had been horse drawn), was completed.

After Rillington the first station was Marishes Road which was followed by the Black Bull (open from 1853 to 1858 to serve Kirby Misperton Hall) where the train would have crossed the Malton – Pickering road around two miles south of the latter. Finally it would have slowed, as it crossed the western end of Hungate, followed by the beginning of Bridge Street, before entering the station.

[130] The station at York was a terminus inside the city walls (between the latter and Toft Green/Tanner Row). To add to the problems caused by the lack of through running, an unplanned proliferation of lines, controlled by different railway companies, had led to a difficult track configuration outside of the station. This meant that trains for Malton had to move forward out of the station in a westerly direction, and then reverse in an easterly, then northerly, direction onto the lines to/from the north. After passing the junction for the Malton (and Scarborough) line they could move forward, in an easterly direction, onto the latter.

[131] Simmons p78, 84 & 86 & Wolmar p76, 77 & 119: travelling was time consuming and tiring (for the majority) as carriage design in the 1850s was largely unchanged from the earliest days of rail travel, lacking suspension, heating or lighting – seating in third class generally continued to be of the solid bench type. Even if trains didn't call at every station, they often had to stop for those which did, or for wagons being shunted in or out of the numerous goods yards. Trains also had to stop frequently for locomotives to take on water, and for passengers to discharge it. Unsurprisingly therefore, trains in the 1850s ran relatively slowly, typically achieving between 20 mph and 30 mph including stops, although 'express' services, travelling at between 50 mph and 60 mph, had begun to be introduced earlier in the decade.

[132] The parish church of Saint Peter was located on a high point between the eastern end of Market Place and the western side of Hallgarth.

[133] Harrison p69

[134] Tourism in the area had begun, and would continue, without the help of the railways although the improved accessibility which they provided further increased the number of visitors. Later, excursion trains, which began running almost as soon as new railway lines opened (Best p222), would bring other tourists.

[135] What was to be Pickering's first police station, which may have been constructed as, or at least converted into, a lock up in 1845 (Whellan & *Post Office Directory* 1879), remains in existence.

[136] Whellan

[137] The kitchen probably had a larder and an enclosed cooking range, which may also have been useful considering the other people who might be in the building at various times.
Decoration, including wallpaper* and soft furnishings, would probably have been more extensive than they'd previously enjoyed. John's increase in salary meant that they also would have been able to buy more and better quality furniture, with clocks, pictures and ornaments increasingly evident.
*Harrison p67: by the mid 1850s wallpaper was being mass produced and so would have been affordable for a family with John's income.

[138] The 'privy' would probably have been in the yard, particularly as potential prisoners had to be catered for. As there was then no water piped into the premises it probably contained a dry closet, using earth and/or ashes (Best p41). At night a chamber pot would have substituted for the 'privy' - prisoners would probably have used a bucket.

[139] A gas works had been constructed by the York and North Midland Railway, on land between Train Lane and the newly opened line from Rillington junction. It produced gas primarily for railway operations but some was supplied for lighting in the town. Domestic gas use was also limited until the incandescent mantle, which produced a bright, white light, was developed later in the century (Best p42).

[140] John George's height was later measured as 5'9" (1.75m) – his father was recorded as 5' 8¾" (1.75m) when he began with the North Riding Constabulary (force average 5' 10¾" [1.8m]: *Register of Constables* - NYCRO MIC 1249 QP).

[141] Taylor p55

[142] The North Riding Inspectors seem to have undertaken a role which shared many similarities with that of the Superintendents (according to the Quarter Sessions Police Committee [*York Herald* October 1860] they performed nearly the same duties) so a *Journal*\* kept later (April 1866 – May 1869) by an Inspector at East Ayton (generally referred to as Ayton), in the eastern part of the Division, is probably a reasonable indicator of what John's 'usual' day might have involved.

The Inspector's typical day involved going on duty at 9 a.m. for two to three hours at the Ayton station before patrolling his local area, or more usually, visiting 'stations' and various other locations in his district, generally returning late in the afternoon. Before going off duty at midnight he usually patrolled\*\* his local area and/or met one or more of his Constables to 'conference'.

The exceptions to his typical day were Thursdays, when the Inspector attended Petty Sessions at Scarborough (where he also regularly 'conferenced' with one or more of his Constables), Saturdays, when he usually finished his patrol after midnight and Sundays, when he tended not to travel and to finish before midnight. He also usually didn't travel if he'd done so extensively the previous day, and/or on the odd occasions when he'd finished in the early hours of the morning.

The Inspector seemed to have managed little time off duty – if circumstances permitted, an hour or so around midday, and/or, a total of two or three hours in the evening.

Other than Saturdays, the Inspector only occasionally worked after midnight, as most 'conferences' were held during the day (mainly between 1 and 6 p.m. although as the majority took place in a Constable's area the timing was probably a reflection of the Inspector's itinerary). The Inspector also 'conferenced' extensively with members of the public, who must have been 'known' as the Inspector found no need to describe their 'positions' in his *Journal* – some were magistrates but Poor Law Guardians, clergymen, farmers and landowners, parish constables and publicans were likely to have been among the remainder.

Being in a significant township, the police station*** in Pickering would probably have required more 'coverage', and therefore more of John's time, than the facility at Ayton - it would be some time before John had any more assistance than the Inspector. John would also probably have been required to engage in more 'conferencing' with members of the public than the Inspector, and also have more non policing activities than him. John also had a second Inspector (with a team) and he'd be expected to support both with events and incidents. He would often be called on, in the same way, to assist colleagues outside his Division (Steeplechases at Malton, Agricultural Shows at Scarborough, Elections at Whitby).

However, as the Superintendent's area was similar to the Inspector's it seems reasonable to believe that the pattern of policing, and of the Superintendent's usual day, would not have been significantly different. It therefore seems probable that, other than Saturdays, John generally wouldn't have worked after midnight but, that like the Inspector, he would have been on duty most of the day and the best part of every evening. This may seem onerous but, if some time off duty during the overall period was possible, it may not have been significantly worse than many other people experienced at the time.

What may have been more of an issue (particularly to Eleanor) was the lack of a regular break from work. The Inspector seems to have had only one full day off in the three years plus covered by the *Journal*, although he was absent for several days through illness on a couple of occasions.

As she was probably the only adult female who was readily available much of the time, and wife of the Superintendent, it seems probable that Eleanor might also have regularly been on duty. Although prisoner's meals were limited to porridge, or bread together with tea or coffee for breakfast and supper [*sic*], with meat and vegetables for dinner (*The First 100* p19), it's probable, with the strict demarcation between the roles of men and women which then existed, that it would have been Eleanor who was expected to prepare these. It's also probable, as the force (like all institutions at this time) was men only – women didn't become substantive members of the North Riding Constabulary until 1946 (*First 100* p41) - that Eleanor would sometimes have had to act in an 'official' capacity. →

In the event of a female (or a child) being brought in to the station she'd probably have searched them on behalf of the officer(s) involved in their 'apprehension', and acted as chaperone, as males were forbidden from unaccompanied visiting (*Orders and* ...), while such 'prisoners' were in the cells.

*As in Essex, every North Riding officer had to complete a daily *Journal*, recording significant activities and discharges of duty. Superintendents also had to produce a monthly *Divisional Journal*.

**Although the *Journal* generally didn't, and wasn't necessarily meant to record all of his duty times, the Inspector's patrols seldom seem to have lasted more than a couple of hours, after which he usually went off duty.

This, together with his relatively infrequent use in the *Journal*, of 'neighbourhood' and 'vicinity of', which imply rural areas, suggests that the Inspector generally confined his patrols to residential areas.

*** With sometimes only a single officer based at a police station, it seems likely that many (and those in Pickering Lythe were probably among them) would have been no more than an official building where a policeman might be found and/or some 'official' business transacted in the limited hours when one was present.

[143] Goodman p315

[144] Goodman p176

[145] The *York Herald* reported in May 1862 that the shops in Pickering were to close at 9 p.m. on Saturdays, having for many years been open until 10 p.m., and ten years later (May 1872) reported that many 'junior' staff in Pickering had expressed their gratitude that a 7 p.m. closing time, established during the previous winter, was being continued over the summer.

[146] In the circumstances it would have been unreasonable to expect any new force to be fully operational immediately on its establishment. Whitby, for example, having been policed under the auspices of the 1833 Lighting and Watching Act, needed to be 'handed over' to the new North Riding Constabulary which, although originally arranged for early January, didn't occur until the beginning of the following month - *York Herald* December 1856 & January 1857.

[147] *The First 100* p7 & 8: the *Cleveland General Association (for the Protection of Persons and Property and for the Prevention of Poaching and Vagrancy)* was one of many 'private' law enforcement operations funded through private subscription.

The 1842 Parish Constables Act had been an attempt by the government to overcome what they'd perceived as a continuing deficiency in police coverage, due to the failure of many counties to establish forces after the 1839 legislation. The Act required lock ups to be provided and magistrates to compile lists of 25 – 45 year old ratepayers, who could be sworn as parish constables, with superintending constables to be put in charge of both (Rawlings p136 & 137).

In Pickering the provision of the lock up on Hallgarth may have been the result of this, and John Heselhurst's appointment, in late 1849, as Superintendent of Pickering lock up, may have been in anticipation of the 1850 Parish Constables Act, which the North Riding adopted (Cowley p70). This Act enabled the Quarter Sessions magistrates to appoint a Superintendent Constable for each Petty Sessions Division (Emsley p48), who'd have charge over any local superintending constables, as well as all parish constables and lock ups (Cowley p70).

Andrew Thompson, the Ryedale superintending [*sic*] constable, mentioned in cases in January and October 1856 (*York Herald* April & October 1856), may have owed his position to the same legislation.

[148] Heselhurst was eventually appointed (*Malton Messenger* February 1857) Superintendent for the then two man (Inspector of Constabulary 1856 – 57 annual report) Richmond Borough force. While this may have resolved John's immediate issue with the Superintendent Constable, parish constables seem to have continued to play a role in the North Riding for some time.

The 1872 Parish Constables Act was to effectively abolish the role, but as late as April 1871 there were reports in the North Riding of their annual mass oath before local magistrates (*Yorkshire Gazette, York Herald & Scarborough Mercury* – April 1858, 1864 & 1871 respectively), with individuals appointed for almost every town and village of any size, including those which were North Riding Constabulary 'stations'. →

This had ceased to be the practice in Essex in 1853, when the police had taken over duties which had previously been the responsibility of the parish constables, as by then the Chief Constable had lost confidence in their ability to discharge these (Capt. McHardy's evidence to the Commons Select Committee, reported in the *Chelmsford Chronicle* October 1853). This followed a specific initiative to involve parish constables in the policing of the county, which foundered because of the many difficulties encountered with what were essentially locally appointed, part time, temporary volunteers.

A case in the North Riding illustrates the type of problem which Essex had probably experienced. At the (livestock) Fair in Seamer, near Scarborough, in July 1860, a North Riding Constable arrested a woman for being 'drunk and disorderly', and asked (the 1842 Act made parish constables subject to the authority of any county Constabulary) two parish constables, who were present, to lock her up. They refused, and as they also wouldn't give him the key to the lock up he had to release her, resulting in them being charged with a failure to discharge their duties. As well as each being ordered to pay 10s (50p) costs (*Stockton Herald* August 1860), they'd demonstrated the lack of accountability of these posts, and the lack of control that others, in this case the county Constabulary but probably before them the 'superintending' constables, were able to exert over them (Melville Lee p298).

[149] Julia may have attended the *National* school, which opened on Hallgarth in 1857 (Rushton *Pickering* p42).

[150] The uniform (and 'accroutrements') suppliers were Hibbert's, in London, who had also served the Metropolitan Police (*Essex Standard* April 1840) and many other forces.

[151] Northallerton, the county town, was where the Quarter Sessions were held and the location they had decided for the Head Quarters of the new Constabulary.

The interviewing of every candidate by the Chief Constable (*The First 100* p17) was a practice which emulated Capt. McHardy in Essex (Woodgate p11).

Although positions in the new Constabulary were probably advertised locally, it's possible that, as in some other counties, a specific date was given for applicants to be at the county town, (or Head Quarters location) if they wished to be considered.

[152] *The First 100* p18: however *Orders and* ... (see below) advised new entrants that they should consider themselves subject to a fifty six day probationary period so, while uniforms etc. might have been issued, appointments may not have been confirmed until some time later.

[153] One aim of the 1856 Act was to extend the structure, introduced by the 1839 legislation, to the other counties, and to the Boroughs (Philips & Storch p229). There was specific mention of the *Rules* being applied in these areas and they were reprinted almost word for word.

As in Essex, Capt. Hill was required to produce instructions for his Constables and Superintendents (and by now Sergeants and Inspectors), and have them approved by the Quarter Sessions before submission to the Home Office. Unsurprisingly, the *Orders and Instructions Framed and Issued for the Government of the North Riding of Yorkshire Constabulary* handbook was copied, with a small number of omissions, additions and amendments, the *Orders and* ... in use in Essex since 1849.

Capt. Hill no doubt took this option as not only would he have wanted to produce a version sooner, rather than later, but the Essex version was a highly regarded, proven document, which had already passed through the approvals process.

The content produced by the largest and highest profile force in the country continued to be a not insignificant element, while that generated in Essex was written by those whose opinions had been sought, and at least partly acted upon, by the government. In his 1857 – 58 annual report the Inspector of Constabulary who covered the Eastern Counties recommended the Essex 'regulations' to any Chief Constables who might be preparing new versions for their forces, and they would no doubt have been familiar to his colleague who covered the Northern Districts [*sic*]. As a considerable part of *Orders and* ... related to the management of the force, particularly financial, at least John would have known what to expect in his new role if, as was probable, Capt. Hill had told him that he intended using the Essex version as the main constituent of his own handbook.

John would also have been familiar with the *Orders and* ... instructions which re-enforced the notion that effectively he'd always be on duty in his new position. →

Constables had to remain at their homes when off duty, although they were permitted to absent themselves if they left a note providing the times of, and an explanation for, this. Superintendents could not leave their Division, without at least communicating the reason to the Chief Constable, and if they did, had to leave one of their Inspectors at the head-quarters station. In Pickering Lythe this may have required the Inspector to then arrange appropriate 'cover' at his usual station, temporarily reducing an already limited force, which would have further increased the difficulties of John absenting himself.

[154] The Inspectors for Kirkbymoorside and Ayton were appointed on 26 and 29 December respectively, while Constables were appointed on 15 and 24 December; 1 and 7 (three) January with the remainder over the next three months (*Register of Constables* - NYCRO MIC 1249 QP).

After the appointment of the Chief Constable, he'd been instructed (*York Herald* January 1857) to obtain the locations preferred by each of the Petty Sessional Divisions for stationing officers. While this may have meant that Supt. Jonas and his colleagues possibly had little choice regarding locations, it would be surprising if the magistrates weren't given some sort of framework to guide them. Practical considerations were probably the determining factor, as in most cases 'stations' had to be close enough to ensure that 'beats' covered everywhere required, and that officers could 'conference', which probably meant them generally being no more than around five miles apart, although it made little sense to locate a Constable anywhere the density of population wouldn't warrant his permanent presence. The availability of accommodation was another issue which would have had to be considered, and in some cases physical factors, such as river crossings or road junctions, may have had some bearing.

Despite there presumably being no suitable accommodation immediately available, and several months passing before a cottage and cells were provided (*Yorkshire Gazette* July 1857), East Ayton was probably chosen as the location for the Inspector because it was on the junction of roads to Cayton and Scalby. It was also the most easterly settlement before a significant descent (and perhaps more critically, when returning, ascent) on the 'main' route to/from Scarborough.

The bridge over the River Derwent, which separated East and West Ayton, was probably another factor, as it may have provided an effective means of controlling the movements of vagrants and the like. A later move to Falsgrave (effectively June 1869), which was much closer to Scarborough (and by then considered part of it - *York Herald* April 1871), probably occurred because the outskirts of Scarborough, which fell in the Pickering Lythe Division, were expanding rapidly and a local police presence was increasingly considered necessary.

Although some early Petty Sessions were called East Ayton, they were held at Scarborough, sometimes with Borough magistrates 'sitting' on the 'bench', as county magistrates also 'sat' on theirs. Petty Sessions reports suggest that the majority of perpetrators appearing in the North Riding (as opposed to the Borough) court came from the county. Special events such as the Fair, hare coursing, and later horse racing, at Seamer, may have drawn potential offenders from Scarborough, but they appear to have attracted them equally from elsewhere.

Despite significant evidence of the generally poor effectiveness of Borough forces, given to the 1853 Commons Select Committee, nothing was reported, over the next twenty years, which suggests that the existence of a separate force at Scarborough may have been a significant issue. The five, soon to be six, constable (Appendix to the Inspector of Constabulary's 1856 – 57 annual report) Borough force was eventually (1865 – 66 annual report) increased in size to a ratio with the population similar to that observed in the counties. The forces seem to have liaised frequently and effectively and operated in each other's areas, seemingly without incident, a practice which had sometimes been an issue prior to 1856.

Oswaldkirk seems to have been provided with police accommodation, and cells (*York Herald* July 1864), but as in some other areas, this had been funded privately and then rented to the county, probably by a local individual hoping that the facility that they'd provided would guarantee police coverage for their area.

*Distribution of Personnel* - NYCRO MIC 1391 QP
*Register of Constables* – NYCRO MIC 1249 QP

[155] As Constables often had to move at short notice, some landlords wouldn't let their properties to them, which led the Quarter Sessions in April 1858 (*Yorkshire Gazette*), agreeing to rent cottages for sub letting to officers.

[156] Almost immediately after his appointment Capt. Hill had inspected the existing lock ups to ensure that they were in order, as he confirmed was the case to the Quarter Sessions in early January 1857 (*The First 100* p17).
By 1858 a circular lock up, near the cross in Helmsley (Rushton *Ryedale* p54), was to be replaced with a new police station (McDonnell p310 - 311), adjacent to the building which accommodated the Petty Sessions.
In Kirbymoorside a new police station, with cells, had been built on Tinley Garth in 1851 (*Kelly's 1872 Directory* & Rushton *Ryedale* p51), which may have justified (or required) the appointment of the Ryedale superintending constable, and it may have been that building in which Andrew Thompson (police officer) was living in March 1851, when three prisoners were also accommodated. The structure remains in existence.

[157] *York Herald* August 1856

[158] *York Herald* January 1857

[159] The 1857 North Riding force of 105 (Inspector of Constabulary's 1857 – 58 annual report) was very different from the 3,000 plus which had been in the Metropolitan Police within a year of their establishment.

[160] The Police Committee agreed the purchase of sixteen horses and ten carts in January 1857 (*York Herald*), and four months later authorised a further six carts (*Yorkshire Gazette April 1857*). This was sufficient to provide a horse and cart for every Superintendent and for every Inspector, although a reference, in April 1858, by the Chief Constable to mounted Sergeants, suggests that the distribution was dictated by necessity rather than rank. However it seems that the Pickering Lythe Inspectors were included, as in July 1857, the *Yorkshire Gazette* reported that land next to the Kirkbymoorside station was to be used for a stable and cart house. The regular use of a horse and cart, mentioned by the Inspector in his *Journal* suggests, unsurprisingly as he had a similar district, that corresponding arrangements had been made when the accommodation at Ayton was being provided.

When the Inspector later relocated, the *York Herald* (July 1869) reported that a stable and (cow) house (for a cart) were being rented at Falsgrave.

[161] The *Journal* suggests that the *Orders and* ... instruction that carts were not to be used unless a passenger was to be conveyed wasn't always adhered to – on average the Inspector used the (horse and) cart on around ten (and the horse alone on almost seven) days each month.

[162] Newspaper reports imply that Supt. Jonas patrolled the streets of Pickering each evening as the Inspector patrolled Ayton.

[163] A copy *Order Book*\* (Ayton June 1857 – April 1863) suggests that Capt. Hill was almost as enthusiastic about 'conferences' as his Essex mentor.

The additional requirements for 'coverage' of a police station, while prisoners were being accommodated, may explain why the Ayton Inspector took his prisoners to Pickering on several occasions – presumably this allowed the 'usual' level of 'coverage' at his station while the Divisional head-quarters was more likely to have been holding prisoners already.

\* Despite *Orders and* ... covering almost every conceivable eventuality and/or circumstance, there was a regular flow of 'Orders' from the Chief Constable, reiterating that 'guidance' or covering eventualities and/or circumstances not previously considered and/or encountered. The 'Orders' would have been copied by the Chief Constable's Clerk to each of the Superintendents, who had to copy them (into their indexed *Copy Book* and) to their Inspectors and/or Sergeants, who copied them into an *Order Book* for future reference, and study by their officers.

[164] As well as directing that townships were to be visited regularly, the *Order Book* also contained instructions that Superintendents were to meet each of their Constables at 'conference' points three nights in a fortnight, Inspectors (and mounted Sergeants) to meet theirs two nights a week and non mounted Sergeants three times a week [*sic*].

The *Journal* indicates that the Ayton Inspector sometimes satisfied this frequency but seldom the timing as most of his 'conferencing' occurred during daytime. →

It seems probable that this was dictated more by the Inspector's typical day than by his Constable's availability, and it's possible that the latter nevertheless also performed full, all night, patrols of their areas. On the other hand, mentions in the *Journal* of:
- the Constable at Ayton being 'conferenced' with throughout the day, every day
- Constables being absent (presumably on duty as they weren't generally permitted to leave their 'stations')
- a significant number of daytime 'conferences'
- Constables travelling to Scarborough, Ayton or other locations for 'conferences' or attending events/incidents (away from their areas)
- considerable variances in the scheduling of 'conferences'

suggest that the Constables didn't necessarily patrol all night, every night. and that the durations and/or their areas may have been restricted.

This is a reasonable belief given that if the Pickering Lythe Constables had patrolled all of the relatively large rural areas, which most of them were responsible for, it's difficult to believe that they could have met as regularly as was desired.* So the patrols by the Ayton Inspector, often restricted in both area and duration, might have reflected what the Constables did, although the latter may have undertaken a mixture of patrols, some of which could have involved full, all night, duties.

Even limiting his 'conferences' to those Constables in his district (see below) would have meant, on average, John meeting one almost every night but, as with the Ayton Inspector, it seems likely that most of his 'conferencing' would have been restricted to the hours before midnight, or at Petty Sessions.

The *Journal* indicates that John had regular scheduled meetings with his Inspectors (and Sergeants) on a more or less fortnightly basis, when he usually also handed over the pay. The exceptions to this were if he must have been otherwise engaged (when he sent a Constable with the pay), if he was attending an event/incident in the Inspector's district, when there were likely to be additional meetings, or if the Inspector had to travel to Pickering for some reason, such as an inspection or prisoner handover.

The location for their regular meetings was usually somewhere equidistant from their respective stations, such as Snainton, unless the Superintendent travelled further into the Inspector's district, although such occurrences were so infrequent that they must have been for a very specific purpose and the *Journal* doesn't generally record what that was. The implications of this are that John didn't generally travel outside of his own district (which considering his responsibilities, limited resources and other constraints is hardly surprising) and only regularly 'conferenced' with the Constables in that district, leaving this responsibility elsewhere in the Division to the local Inspectors.

*'Conferencing' however may at least have been supported by using different routes according to the time of year, possibly in response to the changes in the hours of darkness. Typically, a no. 1 patrol was operated from May, June or July, a no. 2 from August or September and a no. 3 from November.

[165] The 1839 Act had stipulated that Superintendents were to attend every (Petty) Sessions in their Division, but this was probably only practical in small and/or urban Divisions, and may also have been predicated on the expectation of fewer cases, meaning less 'sittings'. The North Riding *Orders and ...* provided for Inspectors to undertake the responsibilities of Superintendents in regard to Petty Sessions, so Supt. Jonas was seldom reported at the North Riding court in the Town Hall at Scarborough, or at the courts in Kirkbymoorside* or Helmsley**.

*With the exception of a period of probably less than twelve months, when it was being rebuilt after being destroyed by fire in November 1871 (Rushton *Ryedale* p49), the Kirkbymoorside court 'sat' in a building called the Tollbooth on the Market Place. (Originally tolbooth [*sic*] was a name, often used in Scotland, for a building which typically accommodated local council meetings, courts, lock ups and market offices).

** In Helmsley another TollBooth [*sic*] (McDonnell p310) accommodated the 'sittings', which alternated monthly between the two towns.

[166] In his capacity of prosecutor John also had to charge those he hadn't personally apprehended. In addition, if a prosecution fell to the police, with a force 'support' structure essentially limited to a Deputy Chief Constable (Superintendent) and a Clerk (Inspector), and with no Crown Prosecution Service, in the event that there was any uncertainty regarding whether and/or what charge(s) should be brought, it seems likely that decision would have been the Superintendent's (or Inspector's).
However, if professional counsel were involved, as was increasingly the case, it's likely that they would have made, or at least been available to advise on, such decisions.
[167] Pickering magistrates had begun 'sitting' every Monday (*York Herald* January 1857) after the 1855 Act led to more judgements at Petty Sessions.
[168] *Malton Messenger* January 1861
[169] Superintendents (and Inspectors) had to provide 'their' Petty Sessions with a quarterly 'overview' of issues which might have local impacts, such as railway construction or new commercial developments.
[170] The requirement in *Orders and...* was fifteen monthly, fourteen quarterly and fourteen annual returns, although others were added from time to time, particularly as new legislation came into force.
[171] In more recent times the detective force would probably investigate serious crimes but it was many years before the North Riding Constabulary appointed detectives, with the earliest reference (*The First 100* p27) to them being made in March 1911. The only specialised assistance (although extremely limited in the early years) which might have been called on at this time, and then only for serious (capital) crime, was the Metropolitan Police (probably through the auspices of the Home Office).
However, if a fatality was involved, several books were available which could be used by local investigators, such as Supt. Jonas. These contained information on subjects such as death through cold, drowning, fire, hanging, 'mechanical' injuries, poisoning, strangulation, suffocation and wounding. Guidelines for identifying victims, and tables, such as of heights to gauge age, and of bone lengths to identify sex, were sometimes included.

By this time the police were also making use of specialists who provided scientific evidence in court (Home Secretary's instructions regarding permitted expenses February 1858 contained in the Essex 1859 *Orders and* ...).

[172] The Inspectors (and Superintendent in the case of Pickering) began the role of Inspectors of Weights and Measures in April 1859 (*York Herald* July 1858), although they were expected (copy *Order Book*) to combine visits to check on the latter with their usual Constabulary duties. This may have been why weights and measures checks only warranted mention in the Ayton Inspector's *Journal*, on average, once every other month. Such a limited frequency suggests, despite the Superintendent having more commercial activity in his area, that the responsibility wouldn't have consumed a significant amount of his time.

[173] Superintendents had to report on the state of the roads in their Divisions to the Petty Sessions immediately prior to the Quarter Sessions, and according to several of the Inspector of Constabulary's annual reports, were also responsible for inspecting bridges. However, a county Bridge Master, who reported to every Quarter Sessions, also held this responsibility so the Superintendents' obligation may have been limited.

The role as inspectors of nuisances may have changed later as the responsibility was taken over (by a Local Board of Health).

[174] Involvement in the provision of poor relief and the inspection of lodging houses had been proposed by the Home Office in 1858, and approved by the Quarter Sessions that year (*Yorkshire Gazette*). According to the Inspector of Constabulary's 1863 - 1864 annual report, sixteen members of the force were acting as assistant Relieving Officers, while twelve were undertaking the role of inspector of lodging houses. This suggests the probable involvement of all of the Superintendents and most of the Inspectors and it seems unlikely that John wouldn't have been among them.

[175] The role of the Inspector(s) of Constabulary was to build on the 1856 legislation and ensure that standards were maintained and improved, and what we call 'best practice' was shared. The reward for forces meeting the requirements of the Inspectorate was that a quarter of the cost of the organisation could be claimed from the government. →

This was obviously an attractive proposition to magistrates in Quarter Sessions (or the equivalent in the case of Boroughs) facing constantly increasing demands from their Chief Constable (or equivalent) and the reluctance of rate payers. The financial incentive (and the wish to avoid censure by the Inspector) also began to make an impression on those Borough forces which previously seemed to have taken little notice of developments elsewhere.

Visits to the North Riding by the Inspector typically occurred over an eight day period, during Spring or early Summer, although year round correspondence was presumably maintained. The Superintendents (and Inspectors) no doubt spent some time preparing for the inspections and then are likely to have had to address any local issues that these generated.

[176] While 171 Indictable Offences were reported in 1870 – 71, according to the Inspector of Constabulary's annual report, 4,307 individuals were charged at Petty Sessions, with an 85% conviction rate. Around one in two of the latter were fined and one in ten imprisoned, or sent to a reformatory or industrial school. Around a quarter of appearances were for Drunkenness or Drunk and Disorderly which had a 95% conviction rate.

[177] Although the police could get involved, broken contracts were generally 'privately' prosecuted - non completion of a (typically year long) contract with an employer (often made at a 'hirings'* fair) was a common occurrence and criminal offence, until 1875.
*'Hirings' involved the contracting of 'servants' for domestic or farm work for the coming year. During this period typical payments locally were £20 - 25 for men, £14 - 18 for women, £14 - 19 for boys and £9 - 12 for girls (in addition to accommodation and 'board').

[178] In April 1860, for example, the *York Herald* reported the fourth attempt to break in to a wealthy household at Hartoft, around 10 miles north, north-west of Pickering.

[179] Cases of what was essentially child molestation or indecent assault of young girls (often female servants) also occurred occasionally. However, like some rapes or attempted sexual assaults, these do not always seem to have been treated with the seriousness which would now be attached and alleged offenders were often dealt with leniently on minor charges, or had their cases dismissed.

On the other hand, if a case was considered serious it was sent to the Assizes for a potentially severe sentence. A judge described a case of rape involving four assailants, in August 1868 in Kirkbymoorside, as one of the worst he'd heard, and after two of the offenders had been tried, and found guilty, gaoled each for ten years (*York Herald* March 1869).

[180] The North Riding was relatively less troubled by 'serious' crime than Essex – the 171 Indictable Offences reported in 1870 – 71 was a rate of 0.77 per 1,000 population compared with 3.23 in Essex while John had been an Inspector. The Coroner may have had this in mind when he made his comment (*Malton Messenger* November 1872) but he was nevertheless regularly occupied. Accidents involving horses, often leading to death, seem to have been almost weekly occurrences. Deaths in the ironstone mines at Rosedale (see below), or on the associated railways, were as common, and there were also fatalities later when new lines, such as that between Gilling and Pickering were being built. Premature deaths, including those of children (commonly as a result of burns/scalds, drowning, being run over by animals or what we know as 'cot death') also seem to have been frequent, although they generated little comment.

[181] Besides the Superintendent, there was only one other policeman then stationed in the town, and if another policeman had been the attacker Supt. Jonas would have been compelled to investigate. As the newspaper demanded an immediate and exhaustive enquiry, if any officer had been subject to disciplinary action as a result, it seems highly likely that would have been reported, but there doesn't seem to have been any subsequent mention of the incident.

The motive for the attack can only be the subject of speculation, but if it wasn't personal, it may have been that whoever was responsible knew that it wouldn't be possible to exact the 'justice' they sought by conventional means.

[182] John was actually moved to Welburn, a village close to the Castle Howard estate, around 15 miles south-west of Pickering.

[183] With the railway crossing at the Black Bull, various gates, and the infamously poor state of the Malton Road, on which the incident occurred, it seems improbable that anything which could be described as 'racing' would have been possible. →

The public houses involved were almost certainly the Black Bull and the Beansheaf, both of which remain in existence, although much altered.

[184] Steadman p119

[185] Consuming alcohol would have been considered, by many at this time, to have been a serious violation of standards. The temperance movement was extremely powerful and very influential and such behaviour was likely to have been considered beyond reproach.

Although several years later, the August 1871 'Brewster' Sessions (annual hearing of applications for renewals of, and new licenses to sell alcohol) illustrates why the behaviour of the Superintendent had to be exemplary.

The Chairman of the magistrates, commenting on John's district, reported that, during the previous year, the Sessions had heard forty four cases of drunkenness (which reflected the 1,121 Drunkenness or Drunk and Disorderly cases mentioned in the Inspector of Constabulary's 1870 – 71 annual report). More serious however were the eighteen felonies, twelve common assaults and four violent assaults which he stated were related to drink (*York Herald* August 1871).

[186] Racing on local roads wasn't uncommon - in May 1864 two men raced along Eastgate, up Smithy (Smiddy) Hill, down Market Place, across Potter Hill and along Westgate (*Yorkshire Gazette*). Ten years later, in July 1874, another two men seem to have used the Westgate – Hungate – Eastgate highway as their course, unfortunately injuring two children playing on Hungate as they did so (*Yorkshire Gazette & York Herald*).

[187] The magistrates, usually local 'gentlemen' with property based income, would have been in regular contact with the Chief Constable, many seeing him at least every quarter at Sessions, but also no doubt often corresponding on matters of concern, which probably included the performance of the local police force. As the collective employer of the Chief Constable they were likely to have had significant influence. This potentially put John and his colleagues in a difficult position as they had to follow the instructions of their Chief Constable, but also had to respond to these powerful local individuals who were used to exercising their authority and expected compliance from those they considered subordinate (Philips & Storch p222 & 223).

[188] The magistrates would at least have been aware of the incident in the George, even if only through the local newspaper.
[189] Half of the eighty eight leavers of all ranks recorded in the copy *Order Book* were dismissed. Three Superintendents, compelled to resign (one after only a short period as an Inspector, having already been 'de-ranked' for drunkenness), were among the leavers after John's offence(s).
After dismissal (or fining), 'de-ranking' was the most common form of punishment used in the county Constabularies (Steadman p108).
[190] The 1854 Reformatory School Act (amended and improved by further Acts in 1855 and 1856) had given magistrates the option of committing offenders, under 16, to reformatories for terms not exceeding five years, in lieu of imprisonment or penal servitude (or transportation) (Melville Lee p352). At least one of the Hill brothers had been involved in establishing such a reformatory, on the Castle Howard estate (*Yorkshire Gazette* October 1856), and after an appeal, at the April 1858 Quarter Sessions, for magistrates to use the reformatories rather than prisons, a notion strongly supported by a *York Herald* editorial, may have wanted to demonstrate their continuing support.
The type of sentences which the Reformatories could be an alternative to, meant that there could be some difficult inmates so it isn't surprising that outbreaks of unrest, some serious, were occasionally reported, and the choice of Welburn (the other stations in the Division were Malton and Slingsby) for John's posting may not have been entirely without other considerations.
[191] Middlesbrough was expanding rapidly following the local discovery of ironstone in the early 1850s.
[192] *Distribution of Personnel* - NYCRO MIC 1391 QP
[193] The North Riding township of South Stockton developed in an area, known originally as Mandale, on the other side of the river Tees from Stockton which was in Co. Durham. Although relatively rural, an extension of the Stockton and Darlington Railway to Middlesbrough, in 1830, had initiated significant development, particularly along the river. While a large and successful pottery had already been established, and may have prompted the 1835 construction of a halt, later to be a station, on the new rail connection, shipping and related industries, such as glass and iron manufacturing and ship building were soon in evidence. →

By the late 1850s significant investment was underway (McLaurin p15, 20, 21, 25, 28, 34 & 35) - in August 1859 the *Newcastle Guardian* reported that three new blast furnaces were soon to be constructed in South Stockton. In January the following year, the Chief Constable reported to Quarter Sessions that the company erecting the blast furnaces was funding an additional Constable.

[194] In 1851 the population of South Stockton was 1,759 which increased to 3,106 by 1861 (*Yorkshire Gazette* May 1861), making it similar to Pickering (*York Herald* May 1871).
The July 1857 Quarter Sessions (*York Herald*) had been told that the Police Committee agreed with a petition from South Stockton for an increase in the size of the police force, and also proposed a lock up for the town.
In October that year (*Yorkshire Gazette*) the Chief Constable informed the Sessions that strikes (implying 'trouble') had occasionally taken place in South Stockton, and might occur again, and that it had sometimes been necessary to call in the Durham County Constabulary (which policed Stockton) to assist.
[195] Middlesbrough was a relatively large town by this time and 'problems' had already led to the county providing reinforcements to the Borough force (*York Herald* January 1858).
Race meetings, including the three day event each August at the course on Mandale Marshes, south-east of South Stockton, were also likely to have been an issue for the town's police force.
[196] While one police record indicates that John was promoted, another states that he was re-appointed (as of 1 September). Similarly, one police record states that his replacement, Mordy, had resigned, but another that he was dismissed for drunkenness. Before taking over from John in Pickering, Mordy had been the Clerk to the Chief Constable. Prior to that he'd spent around ten years as Superintendent Constable at Lofthouse-in-Cleveland where he'd had close links to the local *Association* (*York Herald* January 1857).
[197] John (George) seems to have served around eighteen months in various Divisions before leaving the force.
[198] Rosedale had been a location for ironstone mining since the mid 1850s. The operations on each side (East and West) of the long, wide dale, would have required craftsmen, such as Alfred, almost as much as miners and labourers.

[199] Alfred was living in Rosedale East when he and Margaret married in November 1864, and the following year their first child was born in the dale, although they moved to York, probably soon after that event.
[200] Northallerton was the location of the county's 'House of Correction' (adjacent to the Quarter Sessions building).
[201] *Yorkshire Gazette* February 1867 & *York Herald* February 1868
[202] *York Herald*
[203] *York Herald* March & April 1874
[204] The Chief Constable included animal disease updates in his reports to the Quarter Sessions for years (while the Superintendents and Inspectors did the same at Petty Sessions). The scale of the problem and the degree to which the force was involved is probably indicated by the Inspector of Constabulary making particular reference to it in his 1865 – 66 annual report when he noted, that on the outbreak of Cattle Plague in the North Riding, the Chief Constable had been appointed chief inspector [*sic*] for the county, and that since then the force had been constantly employed in ensuring compliance with the prevailing legislation.
[205] *Order Book* - NYCRO MIC 1391 QP
[206] *Malton Messenger*: Pickering (livestock) market didn't re-open until September 1867.
[207] The 1865 Cattle Disease Prevention Act, brought into force to combat Cattle Plague, by then a national issue, required the disinfection of premises, restricted the movement of animals and ordered their destruction if infected.
*Order Book* - NYCRO MIC 1391 QP
[208] *Yorkshire Gazette* January 1866
[209] *Malton Messenger* July 1871 & November 1875: the Marishes
*Malton Messenger* June 1876: Hole of Horcum
[210] The 1869 Contagious Diseases (Animals) Act applied to Pleuro Pneumonia, sometimes known as Lung Plague, as well as to Cattle Plague. Parts of the Act and of the Cattle Disease Prevention Act could also be applied to Foot and Mouth disease.
*York Herald* April 1870: Divisional Superintendents acting as animal health inspectors.
[211] *Malton Messenger*
[212] *York Herald* April & October 1859

An office had also been provided at Kirkbymoorside for weights and measures related activities (*York Herald* January 1859).

[213] The 'stamp' indicated that the item had been tested for accuracy, and locally would have been applied at the 'stamp', or assay, office on Burgate, in Pickering.

[214] *York Herald*

[215] A Sanitary Board, with responsibility for house drainage, water supply and the removal of 'nuisances', had been formed a few years previously.

[216] *York Herald* September 1859 & *Yorkshire Gazette* February 1861

Watchmen had originally been employed, by some towns and cities, essentially to provide overnight observation and prevent illicit intrusions.

[217] The condition of the roads, who took responsibility for maintaining them, and who paid for that, was a major issue in the district for years.

[218] *York Herald* December 1867 & June 1870

[219] The requirement to report quarterly to Petty Sessions on the state of the roads doesn't seem to have been relaxed following the formation of the Highway Boards, and the police continued to pursue those who didn't maintain them for some time to come.

[220] *Yorkshire Gazette* March 1865

[221] *York Herald* December 1865

[222] *Yorkshire Gazette*

[223] *Yorkshire Gazette*

[224] *York Herald*

[225] By 1840, when there were around 22,000 miles of turnpiked roads nationally, the railways had begun to make an impact and the Trusts, which levied the tolls and managed the roads, were struggling financially in the light of falling traffic. Exacerbating the problem, Parliament had begun to consider that turnpike roads were no longer appropriate in a 'modern' state and, as the Trusts applied for the renewal of their status, applications generally began to be rejected. With Trusts no longer managing them, the maintenance of former toll roads became the responsibility of the parishes through which they passed.

[226] In May 1872 the *Leeds Mercury* reported that using the road required considerable care, and wasn't possible after dark.

[227] Other toll bars were at Pickering (*Yorkshire Gazette* March 1865) and the Black Bull (*Malton Messenger* July 1870).

[228] *Yorkshire Gazette* January 1866: John wasn't the only traveller to have prosecuted a toll keeper in this way. In March 1865 the collector at the same gate had been summonsed for reimbursement by a Pickering man who'd been forced to pay twice for using the road (*Yorkshire Gazette*) and after John's case, in June 1866, the toll keeper, again at the same bar, was charged with demanding payment from a 'rifleman' in uniform, who was entitled to free passage (*Scarborough Mercury*).

[229] *York Herald* September 1871

[230] *York Herald* April & May 1872

The major purchase of stone in 1872 may have been when the Board began what seems to have evolved into an annual order, usually for 400 – 600 tons, of Whinstone, a dark, hard rock, typically used for road chippings, sometimes in conjunction with asphalt. The latter, usually in the form of natural tar, was heated and poured over a compressed layer of stones, or onto a levelled surface before chippings were spread over it.

[231] Later reports suggested that the streets were lit only until 11 p.m. and not at all between the end of April and early August.

[232] *York Herald* April & May 1872

[233] Privately funded officers, such as the Chief Constable was hoping for, had been employed almost since the force had been established (Inspector of Constabulary's 1856 – 57 annual report). They were to become relatively common in the North Riding and from the 1860s typically constituted around a tenth of the force at any time.

[234] *York Herald* July 1862

Staintondale may now seem to be a quiet and isolated area, and an unlikely location to station a Constable, but like most parts of the Riding, and Essex before, many more people lived, and more importantly worked, in rural areas, meaning that there were far more viable communities. The Constable at Staintondale probably also policed at least part of the Hackness area.

[235] The Sergeant's post may have been introduced in anticipation of the Inspector being moved to Falsgrave, and may also have been connected with the inauguration of horse racing at Seamer the previous year (*York Herald* August 1868).

By 1876 a Spring Meeting was also being held, although the main event continued to be in August, which that year required policing by Supt. Jonas, together with forty Constables and the Falsgrave Inspector (*York Herald* August 1876). →

Forty Constables was equivalent to almost a quarter of the North Riding Constabulary, but as the forces reportedly assisted each other with the management of such events, some of the officers were likely to have come from Scarborough.

Compared with most local events the meetings at Seamer were high profile, relatively formal affairs often held over as many as three days, usually with several horses in each of the four races typically run each day. The course was specifically laid out and a grandstand had been built for the more prosperous race goers. It was probably these facilities, and the views across Scarborough bay to Flamborough Head on the coast, and towards Malton inland, that had helped to make the location popular. The vistas were made possible by the course being on the 'level' ground to the right of the road from Falsgrave to Ayton, as it finished the main ascent from the former and before it began a gradual descent to the latter. This meant that the journey of around two miles from Scarborough was mostly uphill and sometimes involved a relatively steep climb. It wouldn't have been surprising therefore if at least some racegoers from Scarborough didn't consider travelling by train to Seamer station, where many other visitors would have been arriving, and using the more gradual ascent from that direction.

Other regular events at Seamer included a (livestock) Fair in July and hare coursing in late November/early December.

[236] The additional Constable may have been introduced after the local magistrates read the comment, by the *Malton Messenger* in January 1869, that as Supt. Jonas only had a single Constable, and a large area of responsibility, he needed some additional support.

[237] Ampleforth was an example of the impact that introducing a Constable from the 'new' police could have locally as a disproportionate number of Ampleforth appearances for 'drunk and disorderly' followed at Helmsley or Kirkbymoorside (*York Herald* April & October 1870).

[238] A Superintendent, two Inspectors, two Sergeants, two Acting Sergeants and sixteen Constables paraded for the Inspector of Constabulary in May 1872.

[239] In 1866 the 'popularity' of the *Police Gazette* led to it being published three times each week, although unsurprisingly that meant considerable repetition across editions.

The importance of the *Gazette* was such that the Chief Constable gave an instruction that everyone in the force was to read and study it.

[240] The 1871 Act superseded the 1869 legislation, which was an early attempt to address the perceived problem of repeat offenders. Among other measures, it required registers to be established of all those convicted of crime (that for England was to be managed by the Commissioner of the Metropolitan Police), and for gaolers and prison governors to make returns of all those they'd incarcerated.

Both initiatives would have vastly increased inter force information flows, and the inclusion of the list, with full details, of all those released (with conditions) from prison, during the previous week, would have made the *Police Gazette* essential reading. Other clauses in the legislation, regarding repeat offending and vagrancy, would also have led to an increased need to seek information via the *Gazette*.

[241] Reportedly (*Malton Messenger* February 1873) the transfer of Ryedale was at the instigation of the Inspector of Constabulary – if so it may have been agreed during his visit in spring 1872.

However, in his 1872 – 73 annual report the Inspector didn't make any comment, other than to record that one Inspector and five Constables (stationed at Ampleforth, Helmsley, Hutton le Hole, Kirkbymoorside and Oswaldkirk) had been transferred.

[242] Ironstone, such as that found across the Cleveland region, which included the North Riding, often contains only low concentrations of iron ore and requires some processing before smelting – much of that at Rosedale was 'roasted' in kilns, using coal, before (it was sent for) smelting.

[243] Hayes & Ruther p28 & 30

[244] *Yorkshire Gazette* March 1874

[245] *York Herald* March 1870: number employed in 1870.
*York Herald* March 1874: number employed in 1874.
The population of Rosedale almost quadrupled to 2,839 between 1861 and 1871 (*York Herald* May 1871). By comparison, during the same period the population of Helmsley experienced only a minor increase from 1,384 while that of Kirkbymoorside fell slightly to 1,788.

[246] There'd only been a Priory in the dale, but with so many abbeys locally (Rievaulx for example was only a few miles away, near Helmsley), it isn't surprising that the suffix came into use.

[247] It was reported (*Malton Messenger*) in March 1864 that a new police station, to accommodate the 'resident' Constable, had been completed at Rosedale Abbey.

[248] *York Herald* April 1871: the criticism by the magistrate led the Chief Constable to admit to the Quarter Sessions that the cells at the station, built only a few years previously, weren't 'fit for purpose'. As Capt. Hill had written to the Rosedale Mining Company, suggesting that they funded premises for his force, as had happened elsewhere in the county, it seems likely that the additional cells, later constructed by the builder (*Rosedale Past. John Spencley, Master Builder* Bert Frank in *Rosedale Historian* no. 17 1994 – 95 Helmsley Archaeological Society), who'd erected cottages and other employee facilities for the Company, were provided at expense of the latter (there are no reports of any discussion of county funding at the Quarter Sessions).

[249] *Malton Messenger*

[250] *York Herald* February 1873: report of the pursuit in January of a miner from Rosedale wanted for theft.

The use of a horse by the Sergeant is consistent with the mention of mounted Sergeants in 1858, and would have been warranted in Rosedale, but equally may be explained by officers being authorised by *Orders and ...* to hire whatever was necessary to overtake a guilty party, so the horse may not have belonged to the Constabulary.

[251] *Malton Messenger*: there'd been a report in November 1857 (*York Herald*) of horse racing at Rosedale and such events seem to have been relatively common – races were held all around the Division, including at Kirkbymoorside and Pickering. However, these local events were generally 'low key', relatively informal gatherings, which often involved only two horses in a single race, although for a time the Kirkbymoorside meeting was more extensive.

[252] *Malton Messenger*

[253] *Malton Messenger*

[254] *Malton Messenger*

[255] Beerhouses weren't 'licensed for wines and spirits'.

[256] *York Herald*

²⁵⁷ *Malton Messenger*
²⁵⁸ *York Herald*
²⁵⁹ *Malton Messenger*
²⁶⁰ First published in 1864, the *Illustrated Police News* was a popular weekly newspaper which featured, sometimes with illustrations, reports of crimes, and criminal proceedings likely to be of interest to a mass market readership.
²⁶¹ An arrest as far away as what is now Cumbria seems likely to have been the result of information being shared, or sought, through the *Police Gazette*.
²⁶² *York Herald*
²⁶³ The existence of telegraph facilities indicates the significance of Rosedale by this time, although the system was already in relatively common use – in April 1870 Supt. Jonas had been summoned by telegraph to the Quarter Sessions at Northallerton, to urgently 'prove' an accused.
²⁶⁴ *York Herald*
²⁶⁵ *York Herald*
²⁶⁶ *Scarborough Mercury*
²⁶⁷ *Malton Messenger*: unsurprisingly 'immoral' characters had been in the locality in the past. In February 1864 (*Yorkshire Gazette*), after exposing herself in the street a woman in Pickering was charged as a common prostitute and given a months' hard labour. Only a few months before the Rosedale case, a female, considered to be a 'loose' character, had been sent to prison for a month after singing obscene songs and being disorderly in the streets of Pickering (*York Herald* March 1871).
²⁶⁸ *Malton Messenger*
²⁶⁹ *York Herald* January 1862
²⁷⁰ *Malton Messenger* May 1862 & *York Herald* July 1862
Throwing the farmer into a river may simply have been to prevent him pursuing the attackers but might have been more malicious, as it was suspected that sometimes robbery was disguised by making an incident appear to be a suicide.
²⁷¹ *York Herald* May 1862
²⁷² The previous November the Chief Constable had given permission for officers to work in 'plain' clothes when it was considered necessary (*Constabulary Memoranda Books* - NYCRO MIC 1392 QP).
²⁷³ Sheffield was around 90 miles from Pickering, close to the most southerly point in Yorkshire. →

Travelling there on foot was likely to have been arduous enough, but having to divert from the most direct route, as the newspaper implied had been the case, would obviously have been worse.
[274] Liverpool was the main port for trans-Atlantic passenger ships, which 'sailed' on a very regular, often daily, basis.
[275] As the Helmsley magistrates closed the court to the public, including reporters, this hearing led to an 'outburst' from the *York Herald* (October 1863), particularly as the paper couldn't understand the reason for the closure. The editorial also considered Lord Feversham's behaviour inappropriate, after he'd 'sat' as (the impartial) Chairman of the 'bench' for the preliminary hearing but seemed to be in constant communication with the prosecution counsel (as the prosecutor?) during the main hearing. Such commentary was unusual, both for the non-deferential tone and for the almost unique nature of the complaints. 'Open' courts had been mandatory for several decades – closing a session is perhaps indicative of the degree of power which particular individuals still held in some local communities at this time.
The newspaper's challenge however may have had an effect, as an October 1870 report of a poaching case mentioned that Lord Feversham, who'd been 'sitting', left the court when the hearing began.
[276] *York Herald* December 1863: this case went to the Assizes due to the violence involved, but night poaching was an Indictable Offence anyway and had to be sent to a higher court (usually Quarter Sessions), whereas local magistrates had jurisdiction over daytime poaching cases.
[277] Penal Servitude, introduced by the 1853 Act, essentially meant a sentence based on physically demanding labour.
[278] Bell p140 & Suggitt p86
[279] Suggitt p88: the Whitby & Pickering 'deviation' line was apparently near completion (*York Herald* February 1862) at the time of the accident as that hadn't been the first time that the cable had parted. In September 1857 (*Malton Messenger*) an iron ore train had run down the incline and derailed, after the cable gave way, and there'd been an incident in October 1861 (*York Herald*) when a mineral train had rolled into a waiting goods train, although fortunately without loss of life or serious injury.

The introduction of the 'deviation' significantly accelerated the service between Whitby and Pickering as the need to stop for the incline, and the attendant delay, was eliminated (although abnormal in nature, in August 1859 it reportedly [*Yorkshire Gazette*] had taken more than two hours to haul a returning excursion train up the incline).

[280] *York Herald*: reports of married women deserting their husbands, often with a lodger, were relatively common, particularly when some sort of theft was involved.

In this case no further proceedings were reported.

[281] The 'chisel' may have been what was often called a ripping chisel (Lock p117), but is now more commonly described as a crow (wrecking) bar.

[282] *York Herald*

[283] Pawnbrokers and second hand shops were the most usual way to dispose of stolen property. Unsurprisingly *Orders and...* instructed that these had to be provided with the details of all such items. In this case, most of the remaining goods were found at a pawn shop and at a lodging house in Scarborough.

[284] *York Herald* October 1864

[285] What was effectively infanticide wasn't uncommon, particularly if servants were involved as an illegitimate pregnancy, or marriage, meant them losing their job. If the death of a child couldn't be proved to be murder, as was likely to have been the case, an alternative charge was 'concealment of birth' (Gray p38 & 69).

Unfortunately for some, such as a 15 year old Thornton (Dale) girl in May 1875, it seems that suicide could even be an option when it came to pregnancy (*York Herald*).

[286] *York Herald* May 1865

[287] *York Herald*

[288] *Yorkshire Gazette* January 1866: punishments such as birching were surprisingly common but this wasn't the only sanction which has now ceased. Although long superseded, even then, in October 1862 it was reported (*Malton Messenger*) that an 18 year old from Thornton (Dale) had previously been put in the local stocks, as a punishment for drunkenness. In January 1868 three prisoners at York were each given twenty lashes of the 'cat' (of 'nine tails') for highway robbery offences (*Malton Messenger*), a punishment which was then common, throughout the country, for such crimes.

[289] By this time the authorities had become conscious of the dangers of physically chastising minors, and a senior officer, such as John, would have been required to observe proceedings.
[290] Not the Welburn near Castle Howard.
[291] *York Herald* June 1868
[292] *York Herald* November 1868 & *Hull Packet* December 1868
[293] *York Herald* January 1869
[294] *Illustrated Police News* January 1869
[295] Crimes were classed as misdemeanours or felonies. According to *Orders and* ... the former included affray, assault, fraud, passing counterfeit coins and rioting. Almost every other offence, including some which now might be considered minor, was among the latter.
[296] *York Herald* January 1869
After the Petty Sessions case in January 1869 (allegedly training the shop lifters), and another in December 1870 (obtaining goods by deception) (*Malton Messenger*), the girl was sent to Sunderland Reformatory. In December 1871 it was reported (*Scarborough Mercury*) that she'd absconded from there for the third time and, as on the previous occasions, had committed a robbery after her escape (she was however returned to the Reformatory).
[297] *Malton Messenger* September 1869 & *Illustrated Police News* October 1869
[298] *York Herald* August 1870
[299] *Malton Messenger*
[300] *Malton Messenger*
[301] The Chief Constable issued orders concurrently with the annual distribution of 'new' clothing, usually to the effect that it was only to be worn at Petty Sessions, during fine weather and/or on Sundays – restrictions usually relaxed a few months later.
[302] New uniform wouldn't have included the 'comb' helmet, which wasn't introduced until 1878 (*York Herald*) when it replaced what was described as a cap. The latter may have been a reference to the 'shako' style caps which some officers appear to be wearing in drawings which appeared in the *Illustrated Police News* in November 1872. However, other officers wore a type of 'bucket' design which was around 8" (200mm) high, gently tapering inwards as it rose to a flattened dome, with a slightly upturned rim running around the base.

Other than the requirements set by the *Rules*, forces could do as they pleased in regard to uniforms and equipment although the Chief Constable's reports to Quarter Sessions suggest that other forces were regularly monitored and the Inspector of Constabulary commented in cases were he considered that uniforms and/or equipment was sub-standard and/or inappropriate.

[303] John (George) married an Eliza Champness from Stanstead (Mountfitchet), but as no relatives were among the witnesses it may have been that none attended, although the location for the marriage was relatively easily accessible by train from southwest Essex.

It was unusual for a bride to marry away from her 'home' parish but in this case could have been because of her parents. Eliza was considerably younger than John (George), which might explain why he seems to have consistently attempted to conceal his age, and Eliza's family might have hoped for a better 'match'. She may also have been pregnant with their first son by the time of the marriage.

[304] The 1869 Wine and Beerhouses Act had already increased police supervision of public drinking establishments (Emsley p75) and improved magistrates' control over beerhouse licences. The 1872 Licensing Act was intended to control the alcohol problem further by restricting 'permitted' hours to 6 a.m. – 11 p.m. (10 p.m. in the Pickering rural areas) or 12:30 – 2:30 and 6 – 10 p.m. Sundays, Christmas Day and Good Friday (*York Herald* August 1872). The Act also provided a structure of fines, using a 'multiplier' for 'repeat' offenders of which there were several in Pickering, where this type of punishment wasn't innovatory. A local man had been given seven days' hard labour after he was found guilty of being 'drunk and disorderly' on two occasions, and a Thornton (Dale) man, found guilty in December 1863 of the same offence for a fourth or fifth time, had been given a month with hard labour (*Yorkshire Gazette*).

[305] *Malton Messenger*

[306] Unless otherwise attributed, the *Malton Messenger* (November & December 1872 & March 1873), transcribed in 2007 by Diana Sadler (assisted by Philip and Sue Coombes, Elizabeth Richardson and Lorelei Smith), on behalf of the *Cropton Heritage Society*, is the source for all 'Cropton' material.

[307] Joseph Wood's deceased common law wife, Catherine Thompson, was the mother of the son (and of two other children in the 'family').

[308] Joseph Wood's reputation for eccentricity may have been partly fuelled by his apparent contempt for 'authority'. He seemed to have failed to attend court (*York Herald* October 1858 & *Yorkshire Gazette* October 1862), having twice been summonsed for alleged non payment of wages. He'd also failed to appear in January 1868 when he'd been charged with keeping a dog without a licence (*Malton Messenger*). Lately he'd refused to pay his rates (resulting earlier that month (*York Herald* May 1872) in the collector of rates for Cropton, accompanied by a police officer, seizing sheep at Joseph's farm, for auction to raise the money owed.

[309] John's search was unlikely to have continued for the three hours he'd once reportedly (*Yorkshire Gazette* August 1862) taken searching a cottage, in the middle of the night, after being called out by a man whose watch had been stolen. (The thief was later gaoled for four months, the first of which was to be solitary - *York Herald* October 1862).

[310] Like her brother Alfred, almost eight years earlier, Julia was married in Pickering parish church.

[311] Contemporary national evidence supported the contentions that in domestic murder cases, victims generally knew their assailants, who were also most likely to have been the last to see them alive, so even if they'd been available, Supt. Jonas wouldn't have had any need for detectives - he almost certainly knew the probable guilty party from the beginning of the saga and only needed help, if at all, with searches.

[312] 'Hirings' occurred several times each year, and in almost every location of significance but the November, or Martinmas event in Pickering was possibly one of the largest and most infamous in the region.

When a 'hiring' was agreed some money was usually paid which together with the opportunity that the day presented for many people, who might not get the chance again for the next 364 days, to have a good time, led typically to what the *York Herald* (November 1863) described as a noisy and uproarious occasion.

As well as more legitimate distractions the sudden relative wealth of often unworldly individuals also attracted cheats, pick-pockets and the like, and not unusually in November 1863 the *Malton Messenger* reported that eight or nine disorderly or suspicious individuals had been incarcerated overnight, following that year's 'hirings'.

[313] A piped water supply had been provided the previous year (*York Herald* July 1871), which in normal circumstances might have made washing a body easier, but in this case the probable condition of Joseph Wood's remains must have made it particularly difficult and unpleasant.

[314] The statement made by Charter also contained a reference to the boy (and the exact wording which had been used and certified in regard to this was examined at subsequent hearings).

[315] In the absence of modern refrigeration (Lock p84), Inquests had to be held as soon as possible, which was particularly critical in this case, as the body was in several pieces and, as it had been buried for several months during the warmer part of the year, was probably in an advanced state of decay. The venue* for the Inquest on this occasion was the Horseshoe Inn, three 'down' Hallgarth from the police station, which also made it convenient for presenting the accused, so that they could give evidence.

* Inquests were held anywhere convenient including private houses (*York Herald* June 1871), and obviously public ones, despite the Petty Sessions having moved away from the latter.

[316] During his evidence Supt. Jonas told the Coroner that, when searching Joseph Wood's house, he'd noticed that a deed (for property of the value of £1,100) was missing. He obviously considered this an important item as the following February the *Bradford Observer* reported that he was still searching for two deeds, and offering a £10 reward (the following month the *Leeds Mercury* mentioned that the documents remained undiscovered). Supt. Jonas's continuing pursuit of the deeds may have been because, had he proved that Charter had stolen them, it might have been possible to make a premeditation case against him.

[317] Wilful Murder carried an automatic death (hanging) penalty.

[318] The location of the discovery of the bones, thought to have belonged to the boy, suggested that the statement that Charter had made, in his cell at Pickering police station, hadn't been correct.

[319] The national press had obviously become aware of the case through the local coverage (*Malton Messenger*) of the searches, and a large number of reporters had converged on Pickering for the Inquest, and subsequent committal hearings. As a result, an additional telegraph 'instrument' and operator had to be brought to the town to cope with the mass of press reports needing to be transmitted, including for *The Times* (29 November), which mentioned that theirs had been sent by telegraph. The *York Herald* commented that even after 8 p.m. on the Friday [*sic*] following the Inquest, 6,000 words had been transmitted, at the rate of 20 words per minute (5 hours).

[320] Adjacent to the Assizes (now York crown court), the Castle prison, sited on what is currently the open space to the side/front of Clifford's Tower, was based on the 'classic' Victorian 'hub and spokes' lay out.

[321] The watch theft was the case which suggested that the Sergeant at Rosedale might have been provided with a horse, as he'd used one to pursue the suspect (to Pickering railway station). The miner, from Rosedale, was later gaoled (*York Herald* April 1873) for two months for the theft (consecutively to two months' for another).

[322] John and Eleanor probably travelled to York more after Alfred and his family moved there but Pickering Lythe seldom produced Assizes cases.

[323] Grand Juries were responsible for establishing if there was sufficient evidence to try an accused, but were effectively later replaced by magistrates' committal proceedings.
In this case the part of the statement referring to the boy, which Charter had given in his cell at Pickering, was made irrelevant by the Grand Jury's decision.

[324] While the wealthy and/or property owning males who made up the Inquest jury had come from the immediate locality, unsurprisingly, for the Assizes (and the Grand Jury) the catchment area was extended to the Riding.

[325] In July relatives of Joseph Wood gathered at John Wood's house, where he and his brothers presented Supt. Jonas with a gold watch and chain, in recognition of his efforts in regard to Joseph's disappearance.

[326] *York Herald* May 1885: the building, in the centre of Lastingham, remains in existence.

[327] Outside the scope of this book, but there may have been some sort of saga (with wider family implications) behind John (George) returning to the North Riding. After their marriage John (George) and Eliza, perhaps surprisingly, seem to have settled in Stansted (Mountfitchet). Two sons had been born and John (George) probably would have had local opportunities, both with his family connections and his wife's, so moving to Yorkshire and re-joining an organisation that he may have left with a sense of disappointment and/or disenchantment, seems unusual.

[328] As well as (Nunnington, Helmsley and) Kirkbymoorside the route to Pickering from Gilling (the junction with a line from Malton to what we now call the East Coast main line) also had stations at Nawton and Sinnington, although by the time of opening only the latter lay within Supt. Jonas's Division.

[329] Generally, level crossing gates were supposed to be kept closed across the railway unless a train was passing but this doesn't seem to have always been the case and the crossings at Hungate and Bridge Street would have been a major inconvenience. More than an inconvenience in some instances. In 1856 a train had smashed through the Bridge Street gates when they were closed across the line (Scales p12). In August 1866, after someone crossing the line hadn't re-opened the gates to trains, the 4:30 a.m. mail train from Malton crashed through them (*York Herald* August 1866), suggesting that the gates, at least at night, were usually open to trains (closed across the road). In December 1871 a 7 p.m. mail train from Whitby didn't stop at Pickering station, and crashed through one of the Bridge Street gates, suggesting, as the gatekeeper had managed to open the other, that the gates were usually closed to trains (open to the road) (*Malton Messenger*).

The following year the Local Board seem to have attempted to persuade the Board of Trade (the government department responsible for the regulation of the railways) to reverse the recommendation of the Railway Inspectorate (presumably made after the incidents mentioned) that the Bridge Street gates should be closed across the road (open for trains), other than on market days (*Malton Messenger* July 1872). The practice recommended by the Inspectorate (who were responsible for investigating all accidents on the railways) seemingly continued, as in late 1886 a report of the death of a local man crossing the line, mentioned that people wanting do this had to open gates.    →

Although their preference was for a subway (*Yorkshire Gazette* December 1886), the incident led the Local Board to reconsider an offer made by the railway company, at the beginning of the year, to provide a footbridge at Bridge Street, as the Railway Inspectorate had also recommended. The need for the Board to take some action probably also arose because the problems at Bridge Street had almost certainly been worsening over the years. The crossing had always been busy in railway terms, not only with trains passing through, but also with the movement of locomotives and goods or freight wagons, particularly those with coal for the gas works. The opening of the Kirkbymoorside connection, and later the line to Scarborough, would have increased movements at Bridge Street further, while probably also impacting almost equally on the Hungate crossing.

[330] *Malton Messenger*

[331] The cause of death given on the Registration Certificate was '*Chronic absess right thigh 2 months. Periostitis* (inflammation of the membrane which covers bones) *right tibia 1 month. Asthemia* (general weakness but can involve blood poisoning and muscle convulsions)'.

A contemporary interpretation of this is that there may have been an initial puncture wound of some sort to the right leg – at that time even the most minor injury could become infected, possibly leading to death, or at least amputation if a limb was involved - which then led to the other issues.

[332] The town was known as Lofthouse – in – Cleveland or Lofthouse (although Loftus was also used), until the arrival of the passenger railway service* in 1875 after which it was known variously as Loftus or Loftus-in-Cleveland.

*The opening of the passenger service between Saltburn and Loftus would have made the journey from Pickering (via Grosmont and probably Middlesbrough) easier than before, even if changes of train continued to be required.

[333] As Eleanor's death was reported by her son in law, rather than by her husband, it's possible that John wasn't with her. This isn't surprising given that he may have only been entitled to eight days' annual leave (*The First 100* p19) and may not otherwise have absented himself from his station.

[334] While the burial occurring only three days after the death and a lack of official records and contemporary local newspaper coverage doesn't mean that there wasn't an Inquest, it seems unlikely.

[335] Eleanor's mother had been around 76 and her father 83 when they died, and at least two of her sisters seem to have been more than 20 years older before they died, so her death at 60 is unlikely to have been anticipated (the age given on the registration of her death was 57 - no checks were made on the age provided to the Registrar).

[336] *Standing and General Orders* - NYCRO MIC 1391 QP

[337] *Malton Messenger* 25 November 1876

[338] The population of South Stockton had more than doubled to almost 7,000 between 1861 and 1871 (*York Herald* May 1871). In October 1862 a lock up was reported (*Yorkshire Gazette*) to be under construction.

[339] *Yorkshire Gazette* January 1866
There were delays in the provision of a new building and, despite the lack of a police station continuing to be a significant issue (*York Herald* April 1868), it wasn't until October 1870 (*York Herald*) that completion was reported although additions and changes seem to have continued for some time (*York Herald* July 1877).

[340] A court at South Stockton was mentioned in a report of September 1867 (*Yorkshire Gazette*). At the October 1870 Quarter Sessions (*York Herald*), it was reported that the rent which had been paid for the venue (local Mechanics Institute) used for the South Stockton Petty Sessions, until the end of 1869, would need to be enhanced for their new location (possibly referring to an extension planned to accommodate them at the new police station).
However, it was June 1875 before the Police Committee agreed that a court should be built next to the police station at South Stockton (*York Herald*).

[341] Police courts were reported at Yarm in March 1871 (*Daily Gazette for Middlesbrough*), October 1874 and November 1877 (*Northern Echo*). They were held in a room in the Town Hall below which, at the time, was the market cross (the structure remains in existence).

177

[342] According to the Inspector of Constabulary's 1875 – 76 annual report the difference in salary between an Inspector $3^{rd}$ class and a Sergeant amounted to only a few pounds.
[343] Wynd pronounced as in winding something up.
[344] Renting the cottage, adjacent to the police station, had been suggested in the Police Committee report of July 1863 (*York Herald*), when the lack of a charge room and accommodation for the adjustment of weights and measures had been mentioned - the buildings, now a private residence, remain in existence.
[345] John Hall was an Inland Revenue Officer (Excise Branch) who worked from an office on Burgate (*White's 1867 Directory*), and who'd lived in Pickering for almost twenty years so would have known John well.
Presentations (*York Herald* April 1877) weren't unusual, as departing officers were often praised in the local press and/or 'rewarded' with some sort of gift by the local community. When Constable Swinburne had moved from Wrelton to Helmsley for example, the inhabitants of the former presented him with a clock, in recognition of his highly respected conduct (*Yorkshire Gazette* February 1865). To some extent, such recognition was 'payback' for policing by consent, a doctrine repeatedly stressed to all members of every force, particularly in areas and/or with individuals who'd opposed the establishment of the 'new' police. However, a more personal reason for wanting to show gratitude was that, at this time, the police may have been the only source of advice, help and/or protection for many people when they needed it.
[346] *Darlington & Stockton Times* October 1877
[347] *York Herald* October 1877
[348] *Darlington & Stockton Times* October 1877
[349] The 1840 County Police Act had authorised that an officer over 60, with at least twenty years (satisfactory) service, might be awarded a pension of up to two thirds of salary, with the support of the Chief Constable and approval by the Quarter Sessions (Scollan p6 & Cowley p112). However, service in other forces wasn't 'transferable' so, although the Chief Constable and Quarter Sessions knew that John had served 14 years and 8 months with the Essex force, his pension of £61.85 was based solely on twenty years with the North Riding and seems to have been calculated using the pay of an Inspector $3^{rd}$ class.

Had his pension been based on more than 35 years' service, and the salary of a Superintendent 1st class, which is what he'd been in Pickering, John might have received more than £113 (salary data from the 1877 – 78 Inspector of Constabulary's annual report).

[350] The Inspector of Constabulary's 1877 – 78 annual report states that in addition to the 193 officers paid for by the county another 23 were funded privately.

[351] Eleanor was buried at East Loftus.

[352] Catherine's father had died six years earlier and with job prospects in Hadleigh probably limited (in 1881 her mother was surviving as a sack maker and there were few alternatives) a job as housekeeper for John was likely to have been considered an opportunity not to be missed.

It seems reasonable to believe that Catherine might have moved to Loftus if Julia had mentioned, in correspondence with family in Suffolk, or with her elder sister in Essex, that John was 'struggling'.

[353] Catherine was actually 30, but could have been 27 when she moved to Loftus. She was unmarried, which although possibly regarded as 'embarrassing' by some, perhaps surprisingly, wasn't uncommon at that time, particularly as employment in domestic service (which may have been where she envisaged her future) was difficult for those who married.

[354] Pensions were not granted as a right until the 1890 Police Act, and unless deemed unfit for service, after medical examination, individuals might continue until they were elderly.

[355] Until the 1931 Marriage Act, the union of a man and his (deceased) wife's niece was illegal, although in their circumstances there was little alternative. Catherine was probably midway through her pregnancy when they married.

[356] They had to apply for a 'Certificate' for the marriage which suggests that they weren't residents of the parish.

[357] The railway network had improved in several respects since the Jonas's 1856 journey to the North Riding. Lavenham had been connected in 1865 (Hadleigh since 1847) and the 'direct' line between Doncaster and York opened in 1871 (Suggitt p119). In 1877 the new station at York had opened which, together with a major reconfiguration of the track layout, would have meant significantly accelerated train movements to, or from, all directions.

[358] A *Guide to Ryedale, including the towns of Helmsley, Kirbymoorside, and Pickering* [sic] had been published in 1872.
[359] *Yorkshire Gazette*
The 1871 and 1875 Bank Holiday Acts had turned Boxing Day, Easter Monday, Whit Monday and (in England) the first Monday in August into Bank Holidays, further contributing to the tourist excursion trade to the area (Best p138).
[360] The line from Whitby to Loftus opened in 1883 (Suggitt p75).
[361] Violet Jonas was born on 31 January 1882 in Burgate – the family might have been staying with a friend of John's, such as John Hall but there were at least two inns on the street – the Kings Head and The Crown, although by this time the latter may have become the White Horse.
[362] *Yorkshire Gazette* December 1882: William Kneeshaw, who died in May 1882, had also lived on Burgate so his home was another possible location for the birth of Violet. William had lived on the street since at least 1861 (with John Hall probably as a next door neighbour in 1871 and 1881), trading as a watchmaker and ironmonger, and *White's 1867 Directory* listed him as also running the 'Stamp Office', so he would have known John (at least in his weights and measures role) for many years. When William made his Will, in March 1882, John was probably in Pickering, and presumably intending to remain there at least for the immediate future (as the timing of the Will and William Kneeshaw's death suggests that the latter was anticipated). When the Will was proved in September 1882, John was described as 'of Pickering' and a 'Gentleman', so presumably at that time was 'enjoying' his retirement and/or life as a new father.
[363] *York Herald* June 1879 & Ellis p5
There were of course many other such attractions in the vicinity and the likes of Rievaulx Abbey were drawing, what we now call independent travellers, from around the country.
[364] The Inspector of Constabulary mentioned in his 1875 – 76 annual report that the Hallgarth station provided very limited (police) accommodation and in 1876 – 77 described the building as inadequate for requirements, so the apparently urgent activity in regard to this issue, following John's departure, is probably no more than coincidental.
[365] In April 1881 the Hallgarth premises were occupied by a Constable and his family.

The 'new' police station and court house no longer exist.

[366] Previously, sheep had been sold on the streets – in June 1872 the Local Board had agreed to the use of their water cart* to clean Eastgate following such sales (*York Herald*), but despite this, resentment towards the sheep market, and the nuisance that it created, had obviously grown over the years.

The produce market sold eggs, butter etc. (*York Herald* December 1883) but the premises were also apparently able to accommodate meetings of more than a thousand people.

It was the Local Board which was effectively to become the local council in 1894.

*The water cart had probably been used around the town since 1860, when a highway surveyor was reported (*York Herald* May) to have constructed a device for watering the streets after the Monday 'fair' (market).

[367] *York Herald* March 1877

It seems that the price charged for gas by the railway company was considered too high. The hope was for a cheaper and more extensive supply - such 'municipal' undertakings were to become relatively common.

[368] *Malton Messenger* December 1887

9 Market Place was next to the Bay Horse.

[369] The capital John had used for his business might have been sufficient to buy some property for his retirement, as he and Eleanor may have originally planned (in August 1874 a house with garden and stables on Eastgate in Pickering was auctioned for £146 [*York Herald*] and in the same month the following year a property on Birdgate sold for £100).

Outside of the summer months, visitors may have been limited and the opening of Pickering castle and grounds, after July 1887, (*Yorkshire Gazette*) obviously came too late to help.

[370] *Malton Messenger* March 1888

[371] 79 was the age given when the death was registered - John may have been within weeks of being 85.

# SOURCES

*Bradford Observer*
*Bury & Norwich Post*
*Cambridge Independent Press*
*Chelmsford Chronicle*
*Daily Gazette for Middlesbrough*
*Essex Standard*
*Hertfordshire Guardian*
*Hull Packet*
*Illustrated Police News*
*Leeds Mercury*
*Leeds Times*
*Manchester Courier*
*Newcastle Guardian*
*Northern Echo*
*The Times*
*Whitby Gazette*
*Yorkshire Gazette*
*York Herald*
all © British Library Board - provided through the British Newspaper Archive

*Darlington & Stockton Times* – Darlington Library
*Malton Messenger* – Malton Library
*Scarborough Mercury* – Scarborough Library
*Stockton Herald* – Stockton Library

Anon KPD Services 2004
*The **First 100 Years** of the North Riding of Yorkshire Constabulary*
Gordon **Bell** Blackthorn 2008
*Whitby, Pickering and Scarborough Railway*
Geoffrey **Best** Fontana 1971
*Mid Victorian Britain*
Brian David **Butcher** Norfolk Constabulary 1989
*A Movable Rambling Police*
T A **Critchley** Constable 1967
*A History of Police in England and Wales 900 – 1966*
Richard **Cowley** History Press 2011
*A History of the British Police*
Christopher **Ellis** Jarrold 2014
*St Peter and St Paul Parish Church Pickering*
Clive **Emsley** Longman 1996
*The English Police*
Ruth **Goodman** Viking 2013
*How to be a Good Victorian*
Adrian **Gray** Countryside 1988
*Crime and Criminals in Victorian Essex*
J.F.C. **Harrison** Fontana 1988
*Early Victorian Britain*
R H **Hayes** & J G **Rutter** Scarborough Archeological and Historical Society 1974
*Rosedale Mines and Railway*

Joan **Lock** Barn Owl Books 1990
*Dreadful Deeds and Awful Murders*
J **McDonnell** Stonegate Press 1963
*A History of Helmsley, Rievaulx and District*
Susan **McLaurin** McLaurin 2005
*Thornaby on Tees in the Past*
W L **Melville Lee** Methuen 1901
*A History of Police in England*
Frederick **Pawsey** Halstead and District Local History Society 1991
*The History of Law and Order in North Hinckford*
David **Philips** & Robert D **Storch** Leicester University Press 1999
*Policing Provincial England 1829 – 1856*
Patrick **Pringle** Museum Press 1955
*Hue and Cry The Birth of the British Police*
Philip **Rawlings** Willan 2002
*Policing A Short History*
R E **Pritchard** The History Press 2002
*Dickens England*
J **Rushton** Blackthorn Press 2011
*The Story of Pickering*
J **Rushton** Ryedale District Council 1986
*The Ryedale Story*

R W **Scales**
*The Way We Were*
Maureen **Scollan** Phillimore 1993
*Sworn to Service - Police in Essex*
Jack **Simmons** Thames & Hudson 1991
*The Victorian Railway*
Graham **Smith** Countryside 2005
*Smuggling in Essex*
David **Speigelhalter** Profile 2015
*Sex by Numbers*
Carolyn **Steadman** Routledge & Kegan Paul 1984
*Policing the Victorian Community*
Gordon **Suggitt** Countryside 2005
*Lost Railways of North & East Yorkshire*
David **Taylor** Manchester UP 1997
*The New Police in 19th Century England*
James **Walvin** Hutchison 1984
*English Urban Life 1776 – 1851*
**Whellan** at al 1859
*A History of Pickering*
Christian **Wolmar** Atlantic 2007
*Fire & Steam*
John **Woodgate** Dalton 1985
*The Essex Police*
Trevor **Yorke** Countryside 2005
*The Victorian House Explained*

essex.police.uk/museum
policehistorysociety.co.uk
riponmuseums.co.uk

# OTHER READING

A A **Clarke** Arton Books 1993
*Country Coppers The Story of the Policemen of the East Riding 1857 – 1968*
Clive **Emsley** Quercus 2010
*The Great British Bobby*
**Essex County Record Office** 1970
*Law and Order in Essex 1066 – 1874*
J M **Hart** Allen & Unwin 1951
*The British Police*
Gordon **Home** 1905
*The Evolution of an English Town*
**Levisham Station Group** 2010
*Pickering to Rillington A Brief History*
Peter **Iliffe** – Moon British Publishing Company 1989
*The First 150 Years*
Charles **Reith** Oliver & Boyd 1956
*A New Study of Police History*
J **Rushton** Dalesman 1967
*Ryedale*
J **Rushton** Blackthorn Press 2003
*The History of Ryedale*
Roger **Swift** Borthwick 1988
*Police Reform in Early Victorian York 1835 – 1856*
Stephen **Wade** Tempus 2007
*Plain Clothes and Sleuths*
Chris A **Williams** Manchester University Press 2014
*Police Control Systems in Britain 1775 - 1975*

# INDEX

This index also applies to material included in the notes, enumerated in the text, which should also be checked when an entry is referenced

Apprenticeship, 13, 14
Assizes, 21, 29, 83, 102, 103, 104
Ayton (East Ayton), 52, 74
Beckhole, 83
Boroughs, 17, 18, 43
Carriers, 30
Castle Hedingham, 25, 26
Castle Howard, 59, 63
County and Borough Police Act 1856, 39, 43, 52
Crimes, 24, 25, 26, 27, 29, 33, 36, 37, 57, 58, 64, 67, 78, 80, 84, 85, 86, 88, 89, 90, 91, 111
Dengie, 31
Education, 12, 13, 34, 51
Essex Chief Constable, 17, 26, 30, 31, 39, 40
Essex Constabulary, 17, 18, 19, 23, 24, 26, 27, 31, 35, 39, 40, 41, 52
Falsgrave, 52, 53, 74
Foxearth, 23, 24
Goathland, 83
Hadleigh, 17
Hallgarth, 49, 50, 51, 66, 97, 98, 115
Halstead, 20
Helmsley, 40, 43, 52, 55, 74, 76, 107
Hinckford, 20, 23
Hirings, 57, 97
Horses (and Carts), 45, 53, 60, 72, 77
Inquest, 29, 98
Inspector of Constabulary, 41, 52, 57, 73, 74, 115
Inspectors, 30, 31, 32, 35, 50, 53, 55, 56, 57

189

Kirkbymoorside, 40, 43, 52, 53, 55, 69, 76, 77, 107
Lakenham, 14
Langbaurgh, 43, 64, 110
Lastingham, 97, 105
Lavenham, 11, 12
Licensing, 60, 78, 80, 92
Lighting and Watching Act 1833, 17, 50
Loftus, 108, 112
Magistrates, 59, 61, 62, 82
Malton, 43, 63, 72, 75
Metropolitan Police, 17, 19, 52
Middlesbrough, 43, 63, 64
Municipal Corporations Act 1835, 17, 43
Norfolk, 14, 17
Normanby's Rules, 18, 19, 40, 51, 52
North Riding Chief Constable, 39, 40, 41, 51, 52, 61, 63, 64, 73, 109, 111, 115
North Riding Constabulary, 39, 43, 52, 56, 57, 65, 73, 74, 111
Orders and ..., 19, 26, 27, 29, 41, 50, 51, 52, 55, 56, 60, 80, 85
Parish Constables, 21, 50, 51
Patrols, 18, 21, 25, 32, 50, 55
Petty Sessions, 21, 25, 35, 52, 55, 56, 78, 80, 87, 107, 109
Pickering, 43, 44, 46, 47, 48, 49, 50, 56, 60, 65, 68, 70, 72, 73, 74, 77, 93, 94, 107, 113, 114, 115
Pickering Lythe, 40, 43, 44, 52, 53, 55, 67, 73, 74, 75, 76, 77
Poaching, 82, 83
Police Gazette, 32, 75, 79
Police Stations (and Lock Ups), 20, 23, 24, 26, 35, 43, 49, 50, 52, 53, 55, 64, 73, 77, 97, 109, 110, 115
Quarter Sessions, 18, 21

Railways, 34, 43, 46, 63, 75, 76, 82, 87, 107, 108, 113, 114
Roads, 21, 44, 45, 57, 70, 71, 72, 115
Rosedale, 66, 73, 74, 76, 77, 78, 79, 80, 85, 90, 102
Rural Constabulary Act 1839, 17
Ryedale, 43, 75, 78
Saffron Walden, 35
Scarborough, 43, 52
Scarborough (Seamer) Races, 74
Sergeants, 30, 53, 63, 74
Sible Hedingham, 25
South Stockton, 64, 109
Southminster, 30, 31
Stansted (Mountfitchet), 33, 34, 35, 116
Sudbury, 28, 29
Suffolk, 11, 17
Superannuation, 111, 113
Superintendent Constable, 50, 51, 65
Superintendents, 40, 41, 43, 50, 51, 55, 56, 57, 69, 71, 74, 75
Telegraph, 36, 79, 93, 99
Transportation (Penal Servitude Act), 29, 83
Uniform, 19, 32, 41, 51, 82, 91, 92
Walden, 34
Welburn, 59, 63
Whitby, 44, 46, 50, 83, 85
Whitby & Pickering Railway, 46, 83, 107
Yarm, 108, 109, 110, 111
York, 46, 101, 102, 113




© Paul B Davies November 2016

Lightning Source UK Ltd.
Milton Keynes UK
UKOW05f2144061116
287008UK00001B/16/P